Women Disorders and Pregnancy

Please consult an expert before starting any medication.

Every effort is made to ensure accuracy of material, but the publisher, printer and author will not be held responsible for any inadvertent error (s). In case of any dispute, all legal matters to be settled under Delhi Jurisdiction only.

Published by
Lotus Press

Women Disorder and Pregnancy

Dr. Rajeev Sharma
M.D., D.Lit.
Dr. Rekha Sharma
M.B.B.S., M.S.

Lotus
PRESS
4735/22, Prakash Deep Building
Ansari Road, Darya Ganj,
New Delhi-110002

Lotus Press Publishers & Distributors
Unit No.220, 2nd Floor, 4735/22, Prakash Deep Building,
Ansari Road, Daryaganj, New Delhi- 110002
Ph:- 32903912, 23280047, 098118-38000
Email : lotuspress1984@gmail.com
Visit us : www.lotuspress.co.in

Women Disorders and Pregnancy

ISBN : 81-8382-066-2

Published by : **Lotus Press Publishers & Distributors**, New Delhi- 2
Printed at : **Bharat Offset Works,** New Delhi

Preface

A women is supposed to be the best creation of God. This is not because of her beauty, but the responsibility that she bears like a daughter, sister, wife, mother, grandmother, etc. Though the body structure of a woman is complex than man, but her duties play an important role.

In this book, I, alongwith my elder sister and renowned doctor of Bulandshahr, Dr. Rekha Sharma, have elaborated some common problems of females like menstural problems, leucorrhoea, anaemia, besides a detailed summary on pregnancy and care during pregnancy.

There are seperate chapters on diet during pregnancy and breast-feeding too.

Hope you all will be benefitted by this book.

With thanks & regards,

Dr. Rajeev Sharma
Srijan - Aarogya Jyoti®
Palm - 11/03, Shipra Sun City
Indirapuram, Ghaziabad (U.P.)
Ph. : 0120-3020206
email : sharmarajeev108@ rediffmail.com
drrajeev@newkamastura.com

Dr. Rekha Sharma
M.B.B.S, M.S.
Gynoecologist &
Ultrasonologist
Dev Hospital
D.M. Colony Road
Bulandshahr (U.P.)

Preface

A Brief About Dr. Rajeev Sharma

Dr. Rajeev Sharma is an eminent consultant of Homoeopathy,Yoga, Naturopathy and Alternative Medicine in India. He has written more than 200 books in Hindi and English and around 1500 articles, which have been published in various newspapers and magazines. He is also a member of the Editiorial Board of the prestigious *Asian Homoeopathic Journal* besides many other newspapers and magazines.

Dr. Rajeev Sharma has written books on ayurveda, homoeopathy, yoga, naturopahty, accupressure, magnetotherapy, water-therapy, massage and aromatherapy, etc.

He has written books on all major ailments like diabetes, hypertension, obesity, stomach and respiratory disorders, E.N.T. disorders, female and male disorders, UTI disorder, sexual disorders, paediatric problems, headache, stress and other mental problems, etc.

The books written by Dr. Rajeev Sharma have been published by renowned publishers of India like :- Pustak Mahal (Publisher of *Rapidex English Speaking Course*), Diamond Pocket Books (Publisher of Osho literature, *Greha Laxmi, Cricket Today* and *Sadhna Path*), B. Jain Publisher (largest publisher of book on homoeopathy and alternative medicine in India). Jaypee Brothers Medical Publishers, Crest

Publishing House, and Manoj Publications.

Dr. Rajeev Sharma is Medical Advisor to Ralson Remedies (a homoeopathic medicine manufacturer), and Dixit Pharmacy (Ayurvedic Medicine Manufacturer), Medical Examiner at the Life Insurance Corporation of India and M.O. in U.P. Govt. He has received several prizes for his outstanding achievements. He has been awarded the *Best Author prize in Hindi* by the Home Ministry and Ministry of Health and Family Welfare, Government of India and *Sarjana Puraskar* by U.P. Hindi Sansthan, Lucknow. He has delivered talks on All India Radio and lectures on Alternative Medicine in various Government and Non-government Organisations. He has written Advertising scripts for the products of several companies.

Dr. Rajeev Sharma is also a social activist. He has worked a lot against Drug Abuse and prevention of AIDS. Now-a-days, he is working on a project to check the population growth of India with an NGO called 'Nav Chetna Manch'. He has worked for pollution control and human rights too and has received the World Human Rights Promotion Award. His name has been published in *LIMCA BOOK OF RECORDS 2005*. He has developed two websites too — www.newkamasutra.com; and www.indiaalive.net

Contents

About the Author 5
Preface 7

WOMAN DISORDERS

1. Female Sex Organs 13
2. Childhood and Puberty 24
3. Menstruation (Menses) 29
4. Metrorrhagia and Menstrual Colic 33
5. Menopause or Critical Age 38
6. Anemia in Ladies 43
7. Leucorrhoea–A very common Problem 46
8. Hysteria and Hysteralgia 50
9. Sterility/Infirtility/Frigidity 53

PREGNANCY

10. Marriage and It's Benefits 61
11. Tests Used in Pregnancy 64
12. Pregnancy and its Symptoms 65
13. Precautions During Pregnancy 70
14. A Tabulated Chart to Confirm Pregnancy by Symptoms 80
15. Antenatal Care 81
16. Some Sure Sysmptoms of Trouble During Pregnancy 85

17. Exercise During Pregnancy 91
18. Fetal Development and Emotions 98
19. Physical and Emotional Changes in the Woman 108
20. Infertility Problem ? When to Start Worrying 118
21. Artificial Insemination/Test Tube Babies and Surrogate Mothering 124
22. What to do for Good Birth Experience 129
23. Care During Delivery 139
24. Diet for the Pregnant Woman 142
25. Breast Feeding 149
26. Food Supplement for Infants 153
27. How to Feed a Young Infant 155
28. Feeding of Infants During Ailments Immunization 159
29. Essential Nutrients for All 162
30. Contraception 165
31. Smart Women are More Fertile 169

Women Disorder

Female Sex Organs

Most of the organs in a woman are not visible to the naked eyes, particularly those which actually are helpful in reproduction. All her external and internal organs can be categorised as follows :

Internal Organs

- Libia Minora
- Vagina
- Uterus or Womb
- Ovaries
- Fallopian Tubes
- Urethra
- Cervix

External Organs

- Labia Majora (Vulva)
- Clitoris
- Uretheral opening
- Pubic hair or hairy eminence
- Anus
- Breasts

Internal Organs

Female organs are more complicated than the male organs. A brief description of all the major female organs is being given below.

Vagina

It is like a canal or tube that extends from vulva to cervix (neck of the uterus) and measures about from $3\frac{1}{2}$ to 4 inches in length, when in its normal and relaxed position. It is a gateway to admit insertion of penis and is capable of expanding so as to adjust itself to the length and thickness of the penis. Vagina has manifold functions to perform such as :

- ☞ Allowing the entry of male organ (Penis) and not letting the same ruptured or injured due to its cosy and flexible walls by producing a liquid which keeps the penis and vagina saturated, moistured and lubricant.
- ☞ It receives male sperms and carries them towards uterus (womb) to meet ova.
- ☞ It allows passage of menstrual and leucorrhoeal flows.
- ☞ Through this tube the child passes out.
- ☞ Its flexible walls secrete a fine fluid that is a great cleanser and moisturiser.
- ☞ Despite its narrow passage but due to its capacity of contraction and expansion, it can accommodate even a large-sized penis.

In certain cases, particularly in young girls, accommodation of even an average size penis is a problem, due to the fact that vaginal walls neither expand nor excrete vaginal moisturiser. But, as the time passes, it regains its lost capacity.

Womb or Uterus

Uterus is a pear-shaped muscular organ that resembles almost the shape of an infant's feeding bottle. In a virgin its length is about 2-3 inches and width about 2 inches. Its muscles expand with the growing size of the child during the course of pregnancy. It is situated at right angles to the vagina. It has a opening or neck which is called-cervix, and its upper part is connected with two fallopian tubes that emanate from the ovaries.

Strong ligaments of the pelvis support the uterus. Its upper end is heavy and directed towards the front of pelvis whereas cervix (small end) opens into the vagina and closes its upper end.

It is endowed with so much of elastic-power that it starts secreting after the child-birth and gradually returns to its original position. Its muscles are so powerful that they help the baby to move out. From the inception of formation of baby till the delivery of the baby the vagina retains sufficient amount of food supplies to nurture and nourish the child.

Ovaries And Fallopian Tubes

The function of ovaries is like that of male testes. The upper end of the womb is joined by the fallopain tubes—each fallopian tube measuring about 5½ inches in length. Chief function of these fallopian tubes is to conduct the passage of ovum from ovaries to the uterus, which is attained through contractibility of the tubes' finger like fringes called of 'Fimbria' whose sweeping motion remains only in one direction that helps the egg cells to move in a particular direction i.e. from fallopian tubes towards the womb. 'Ovulation' is the technical term used for fertilization of an egg-cell (ovum) which takes place, in some cases, during the time of its journey (movement) from the fallopian tube. When an egg gets fertilized, it moves down the fallopian tube towards the uterus.

Vulva

These two fleshy folds (which are covered with hair) are the two outer lips (labia majora) but, when parted with the help of fingers, they look like inner lips (called labia), inner side of which (labia) are covered with mucus membrane.

These inner labia are the seats of sexual excitement and sensation. During the course of conjugation those lips are continuously massaged by to-and-fro movement by rubbing action of the penis.

Clitoris

Its male counterpart is glans-penis of a male. It has a erectile tissue and gets into erectile position when touched by tip of male penis or when massaged gently by thumb and adjoining fingers. Clitoris is covered from above by a hood of skin and is a highly sensitive organ which is a trigger point in sexual stimulation. It is an epicentre of emanance of sexual feeling that initiates from this organ and sends the female body into volleys of sexual excitement. The sexual excitement, generating by caressed fondling and gentle massage, permeates in the whole female body, when vaginal juices start secreting giving a clear indication to man that the lady is ready for intercourse. As blood circulation in the clitoris increases, it attains an erectile position and its form assumes, in certain women, the size of a thumb or else a mini penis.

Since clitoris is a highly sensitive organ it is amenable to bacterial infection. Hence, it must be kept free of any unhygienic effect lest infection spreads to surrounding organs. In western countries, clitoris stimulation is a highly valued sexual method.

Hymen

Unfortunately, for the newly-married girls, hymen is still considered to be a symbol of her chastity and virginity for the simple reason that if a married lady, on first meeting (sexual intercourse) with her husband, does not pass blood, her virginity is suspected upon and an accusing finger raised against her. In a few cases, it is taken as an excuse for break-up or divorce.

The hymen is a thin membrane that lies just below the urinary passage. During the first intercourse the hymen gets ruptured, resulting in mild pain, soreness and bleeding. In young girls, it gets ruptured during pre-marital stages even, due to falls, jerks, jumpings, playing games, performing some rigorous work or performing athletic feats, etc. Certain hymens are too tough to be broken (ruptured) even after a number of intercourses, but a soft hymen is torn apart by penile thrusts.

More About Ovaries and Fallopian Tubes

There is no existence of fallopian tubes in a male but male testes are compared to female's ovaries. Fallopian tubes join upper end of the uterus and their chief function is to conduct ovum from the ovaries to the uterus. But for the ovaries and fallopian tubes, there would have been no production of ovum which, at the time of ejaculation, establishes contact with the male sperm. An ovum is born when it takes up its journey from the tube to the uterus. In some ladies, fallopian tubes are so thick, rigid and hard, and narrow that eggs can neither enter the tube nor travel to uterus. Narrow passage of these tubes also hinders feeding to the foetus. Since the ovum develops in these tubes, the aforesaid inhibitory factors stand out as obstacles.

Atorphy and narrow passage should be fully treated so that this defect is removed in time. Hormonal function of ovaries is far more complex as compared to male testes. Hormonal secretions govern personality and make-up of a lady and her female character. Ovaries also govern normal functioning and various other chemical substances that control reproductive functions. If ovaries are removed at the time of puberty or even earlier, female development gets drastically changed.

The egg-cells start to mature from the time of onset of menstruation.

Breasts

The first organ that distinguishes a female from a male is her breast which indicates womanhood of a lady. A lady who has undeveloped breasts is called a 'flat-breasted' lady. Though breasts have no role to play in reproduction of a child, it is the most significant part of her body, next only to her clitoris, to elevate sexual arousal of a lady. Nipples are generally of light brown colour and the round area, around the nipples, is known as 'areola'. Nipples form one of the most sensitive erogenous zones on a woman's body. They are directly connected with her other sex organs. Most sensuous sexual desire reaches its zenith when nipples are touched, squeezed and sucked and they are a direct source of sending even a 'cold' lady into sexual ecstasy. A man always loves to handle, caress and suck his woman's breast-nipples.

Erectile, elevated, rounded, muscular and shapely breasts are indicative of a woman's beauty and add to her personality. If there are endocrine gland disorders, breasts may enlarge or even remain miniature but, in either case, it does not constitute a disease. Breasts consist of skin, fat matter, milk producing glands, a tube that stores milk within, nipples and areola. Breasts start to develop in size, volume and shape. As a woman conceives, her breasts enlarge so as to accommodate milk production. In certain women breasts get so much filled with extra quantity of milk that milk needs to be squeezed out or else it wets and saturates the bra. These days, small breasts can be easily enlarged by way of plastic surgery or else by using padded bras. There are about twenty ducts and each of them helps to produce milk. Before these ducts open into a nipple, they enlarge and broaden to accommodate storage of milk. There is no denying the fact that breast-feeding is, by far, the safest and cheapest source of feeding a child.

If breasts are not tied with a bra, they hang down and become pendulous, unshapely and flabby. Morever, large breasts are not easy to manage, as they spoil figure of a lady. Hence, due care and hygiene of breasts is an important part of any woman's personal hygiene. Sagging and pendulous breasts do not delight a male also and, in some cases, they are driven away from sexual pleasure.

In order to keep healthy and attractive breasts, the ladies should take following measures, viz.

- Use only such bras which are neither too tight nor loose. If the bra is extra tight it will hinder respiratory process but if too loose, their breasts will hang and sag and lose their shape lines.
- Wash nipples and area around nipples daily while taking bath and if there is any injury, eruption or ache, get the same treated.
- Any hardness of in any part of breast needs to be investigated. If there is a growth which is benign but is painless, there is no occasion for any anxiety but when tenderness or pain is felt, it must be got examined.
- Lactating mothers should keep their nipples absolutely free from any infection lest the child's health gets adversely affected by transmittance of infection to the child.
- Even after feeding your child, make it a habit to wash your nipples each time but do not apply any medicine in case of any disorder. You should not breast-feed your child as long as your infection persists.

Let out a few drops from your nipples before feeding your child. Make sure that the child doesn't get suffocated due to, extra milk flow from the breasts. If that is the case, a gap should be provided when the child is sucking milk—it will provide the child much needed respite and gap.

Conception and Pregnancy

If all the organs of generations of a woman are in perfect condition and functioning normally, she will be able to conceive and can be impregnated. Certain ladies are immune to sexual act but not infertile.

Impedimental Factors in Conceiving

(i) Some chronic debilitating ailment and general ill-health.

(ii) Innate hatred for the male member—as a community occasioned by some frightful events in early childhood.

(iii) Male dominance and an uncaring attitude towards his female partner.

(iv) Irregular menstrual periods.

(v) Pseudo-psychic phobias as to abnormal penile length or barbarity of male.

(vi) Chronic leucorrhoea.

(vii) Habitual miscarriage/Abortion and weak uterus muscles.

(viii) Mental tension, cares and worries of daily life, socio-economic and psychological factors.

(ix) Anaemia and poor quality of blood and excessive bleeding during menstruation or due to some other factor(s).

(x) Elderly female but young male partner or vice vessa, i.e. too great disparity in age.

(xi) Embedded hallucinations, misconceptions.

(xii) Excessive sexual indulgence in pre-marital period.

(xiii) Untidy, unhygienic, filthy ladies who suffer from foul body odour and sweat fail to attract their partners and, thus, drive them away from sexual act.

(xiv) Personal ego, sense of superiority or feeling of belonging to a family of higher financial and social status often prove inequitable partners and treat their husbands as inferior, less privileged ones.

(xv) Ladies who are too sexy, arrogant, haughty, and self-confined, fail to have any successful sexual rapport with their husband, and cause premature ejaculation to their husbands -simply to let them down or prove that they (men) are really impotent and incapable of satiating her sexual hunger. The situation could be the other way round also when men ejaculate their female partners by oral sex or unnatural methods.

(xvi) Ladies who remain too much engrossed in the domestic jobs, remain busy looking to the comforts of other family members, find, generally, no pleasure in sex and, if at all they are forced to participate in sexual intercourse, their mind wanders elsewhere and, thus they perform it merely as a formality or ritual.

(xvii) Girls whose vaginal depth is not deep and wide, wouldn't admit male penis inside their vagina for fear of being torn apart.

(xviii) Working ladies are not much interested in intercourse for obvious reasons. Their choice may fall,elsewhere. if a colleague of theirs is more handsome, accommodative, jolly, prosperous, better placed as compared to their husband. There could be good many exceptions also when despite heavy and odd office working hours and jobs, the lady may not be enamoured by any one of the above mentioned factors in other men. Same is, often, the case with men also.

(xix) Unless there is meeting of body and mind, conception cannot take place and if it takes place, it doesn't terminate in a successful pregnancy. Conception can take place only when both partners enjoy and appreciate each other's sentiments.

Actually in certain cases, birth of a girl is not considered auspicious and ladies who fail to bear male children are considered as ominous; hence despised and looked down with scorn and contempt. Fear and apprehension mentally drive a young lady not to have coitus, or they, at least, avoid it. It is very difficult to tell whether a lady will bear a male or female child, These days, pregnancy test on determination of sex of the foetus is carried out. If it is the male child, the future mother is looked after very well but, if the results show coming of a girl, the lady is either compelled to abort herself or else she herself opts for abortion lest she has to bear the brunt of family members' wrath and displeasure. This is really a social crime, as repeated abortions/ miscarriages, whether natural or imposed, create certain long-standing problems which, quite often, prove even fatal.

Such retrogressive and damaging customs, ideas, and misconceptions must not find any place in a civilised society. We have to reverse this trend. Let us not forget, it is the girl who becomes a mother and if girls are killed, it tantamount to infantile genocide. Such an approach is also an affront to our social and family culture. It we go on reducing the number of female children, how shall the male progeny will come into being?

Use of Contraceptives and Family Planning

Concept of Family Planning has been misinterpreted—it simply means that there must be a considerable gap between the birth of two children, and that the second child should be born only when the first child has reached the age of 5 years. Repeated birth of children or even frequent abortions spoil a mother's health, apart from shattering family peace.

The mother, no doubt, needs a gap of at least 3-4 years between the first and second deliveries. Frequent arrival of infants have a bearing on mother's health and economic status of a family. Hence, there is nothing wrong in resorting to methods (whether natural or artificial) that help to contain number of children.

I am personally of the opinion that 2-3 children, with reasonable gap of 3-4 years, between birth of two children is an ideal,number for any family. It is immaterial whether all are boys or girls or both. Emphasis is not on sex but on number of children. Parents who do not have sufficient capacity to look after the health, education, general well-being, and marriage etc. of their wards lose the moral right to own any child. It is an unjust and imprudent act to go on rearing children, without ensuring proper safeguards for their all-round development.

As for birth-control operation is concerned, it is the male who should use condoms of good quality, resort to ejaculation by hand-pollution or by excreting semen outside the vagina or have oral coitus or else should go for a reversible/ irreversible operations.

There are certain creams, foams, Copper-T, Oral Pills, Intrauterine Device (IUD), Diaphragm Rubber caps (available in various sizes) to be used by ladies. But, I am not in favour of a lady's going for any one of the birth control measures because, despite all cautions, there are always chances of even quite serious complications. Hence, only men should go in for birth-control measures.

Let me dispel a myth: there is no difference in the intensity and volume of sexual joy and pleasure, if a man uses/ undergoes some birth-control device. If, at all, there is any difference, it is a fall out symptom of mental phobia. Ladies who breast-feed their babies, it is claimed, are immune from conception as long as they breast-feed their babies.

Anyway, choice of a specific method depends on an individual's personal liking and choice, and different ways, means and devices can be worked out according to reciprocal convenience and concurrence of both the partners.

Childhood and Puberty

Parents should ensure that a girl child is not neglected or ignored, nor treated as a third grade person. The tendency needs to be condemned for the simple reason that boys should not be given any preferential treatment as compared to the treatment given out to a girl child. If parents neglect their daughters, others will also not take kindly to her nor have any sympathy and concern for her.

Family is the eternal home of virtues and inculcation of actual habits. When growth period is marred by imprudent discriminatory behaviours, a child's all-round development gets adversely affected.

Childhood

Following suggestions may be tried to keep your girl child in normal mental and physical frame -

- Never discriminate on the grounds of showering favours and meeting (just) demands.
- Never rebuke your daughter nor allow your male children to deride, demean and insult her.
- Give her full freedom as to her choice of food, dress, play and timings.
- Do not supress her freedom of expression, even if oblique, nor outrightly reject her, even reasonable

demands. If you do so, you will simply retard her mental faculties.

- Never condemn, deride, insult or rebuke her in the presence of others, as it will take away her initiative and blunt her genius.
- Provide her with all playthings, toys, means of entertainment. At least she must be provided with, what is offered to her brother.
- Dining-table should be utilised as a joyous occasion for a get-together when no problems should be discussed. Let the child play when she plays and eat while she eats.
- Keep a watchful eye over your daughter's friend circle, the places she visits, the hours she spends at school and home. The parents must lend her a helping hand in solving her study-related and personal problems.
- Never engage your young one in arduous domestic chores nor expect her to sacrifice her leisure and rest time. She should be taught to spend proportionate time in light homework, eating, relaxation, entertainment and rest. None of the aspects should be neglected or sacrificed for the other.
- Have your daughter medically checked up after every 2-3 months and even earlier if the situation demands.
- Do not let her venture into hazardous sports, activities, in handling electrical and mechanical gadgets, fire, water, gas etc. She should gently be guided about the dangers involved therein.
- Never criticise you daughter's friends and classmates nor her habits, choice for colours, dress, etc.

Your parental care, love and affection will serve her as an excellent tonic, and will ensure her all-round progress and growth. Remember, a happy and healthy girl child means a happy and healthy family. It is the girl who develops into a young woman, and finally to motherhood. The mothers must not forget that they too, had passed through the same stage from which their daughter is passing now. Your approach should be persuasive, friendly, motivating and educative—there being no other option.

PUBERTY

The term simply implies to onset of sexual maturity when a girt steps into her youth and is in a position to menstruate. Puberty occurs in both the sexes when changes in body organs surface and appear. In young girls, the following symptoms/characteristics will herald onset of puberty.

- ☞ Growth of hair in arm-pits and pubes
- ☞ Matured voice and deepening of voice
- ☞ Prominence of Nipples and elevation thereof
- ☞ Tingling sensation on slightest touch on clitoris, labia majora, nipples and pain in nipples with tenderness.
- ☞ Flushings on face or reddening of face and eyes on mere sight of opposite sex, and an urge to establish rapport, with the boys.
- ☞ Taking delight in amorous and sex-related talk, matters, pictures, movies, periodicals, photos etc.
- ☞ Bleeding form Vagina (onset of menstruation) is an, amazing event in young girl's life.
- ☞ A sense of Narcism (i.e. when one begins to love one's own self) develops.
- ☞ Breasts start to protrude and there is roundness around the nipples which assume a light brown colour. Enlargement of breasts is a novel experience for the girls who walk stoop-shouldered lest others notice the change.

Puberty is the most amazing, yet tantalising, experience for the girls as bodily changes take place. It is but natural for the young girt to get hypernervous. In certain girls, breasts enlarge at a rapid pace, when use of bra becomes a necessity. In order to overcome elements of mental trauma and surprise, an elderly lady should take the initiative of educating the girl, in details that misgivings do not surface nor is there any occasion for confusion.

How to educate and guide a girl at puberty stage

Physical changes, onset of menses with resultant bleeding and attendant complaints before, during and after menses, should not be overlooked by elderly ladies. In fact, girls are generally, fully informed due to dissemination of relevant knowledge by books, audio-visual media and mutual discussions between senior and junior girls.

Elements of hesitancy and mental reservation should be given a go-bye and, in this respect the mother or the senior sister or sister in-law or some other female member has to take upon herself the onus of guiding the young girl. Following methods/devices may be adopted for the purpose viz :

- She should be frankly told that all young girls have to pass through pubic stage and there is nothing new or surprising.
- Let her be provided with some literature and induced and motivated to study even each and every minute detail so that her fear and psychosis disappear.
- She should be educated about common complications like bleeding from vagina, amount of menstrual blood, pain in back and head, with occasional mental agitation, paleness of face, cold extremities and run-down conditions, all of which subside as soon as menstrual flow ceases.
- Personal hygiene factor bears utmost importance and it is a myth that menstruating lady should not take bath, lead a sedentary life, give up studies, eat less or perform no physical activity at all.
- The girl must not conceal any psychic or physical problem from her mother or doctor as, it will simply lead to further complications which, if allowed to prolong, may permeate into permanent problems.
- They should be guided towards use and change of sanitary towels and wash her vagina and outer parts with some bland and non-irritating (medicated) water.
- The girls should not wear tight bras lest shape and

development of their breasts gets adversely affected, nor should extremely loose bra be used (to avoid any shabbiness or uneasiness).

☞ The girl and her mentor/guide should have close rapport and there should be no inhibition or hesitancy either in disclosing problems or in suggesting a way out.

☞ Puberty is a common occurrence and there is no cause for any alarm or surprise over changes in body organs and development thereof.

Menstruation (Menses)

Puberty is a forerunner of menses which means that the young girl has now reached a stage when she can conceive. Since the event is unique in their life, they are liable to get confused, worried and nervous with factors that can be easily resolved by judicious and sympathetic guidance. Generally, it is difficult to draw a dividing line between puberty and menstruation because onset is almost simultaneous in most of the cases, though there are exceptions too. Onset of menses is a clear indication that the young girl is ready to become a mother, provided other factors are also favourable and congenial. No girl could ever become a mother if she does not menstruate which is a first step towards motherhood.

Facts about Process of Menstruation

- It is a natural 'process : a novel and sudden experience for the girls who have entered the threshold of youth, and is an indication pointing towards their impending motherhood.
- It is a natural episode and all fears, doubts, or misgivings should find no place.
- Normally a girl of 11-14 years or even over 14 years, starts passing blood from her genitals on every 28th day of each month and bleeding continues for about 4 days. These are normal parameters which often vary,

as every girl is a law unto herself. To explain this point further, it is necessary to note that certain girls menstruate even 4 days or may cease even earlier. So, earlier or delayed onset of menses should neither cause any alarm nor any confusion. Further, menstrual flow may last a little earlier or later which, in most of the cases should be taken as a normal course, provided there are no other disturbing symptoms.

☞ There is no set rule regarding quantity of blood passed (which is about 12 ounces in a total period of 4 days) but exceptions are still there.

☞ Excessive passage of blood and quantity of blood passed may vary in certain individuals. If excess amount is passed, the doctor should be consulted and remedial steps taken. But, if the flow is scanty, or if the onset is normal but flow of blood is either interrupted or even stopped, it calls for medical advice.

☞ Menses may be either
Scanty
Retarded
Excessive
Delayed
Premature, or
May cease after onset or
May stop and resume after a few days, or
May be painful

All the forementioned states constitute a disease (in each case), the causes of which must be got investigated and corrective/remedial steps taken in time.

Most of the ladies may show any one, some or all of the following symptoms viz.

☞ Aching or heaviness of head.

☞ Backache and pain in pubic region. Pain in lower abdomen.

☞ Sensation of weight in waist and thighs.

☞ Pruritus and/or excessive sweating.

☞ Palpitation.

- ☞ Agitated and withdrawn behaviour.
- ☞ Disclamation to do any mental or physical activity or else tendency to take rest.
- ☞ Run-down feeling and general weakness, pallor, and low spirits.
- ☞ Revulsion from coitus or, in rare case, intense and irrepressible desire for coition
- ☞ Blemishes, blackheads, black patches on face, or Acne (Facial pimples)
- ☞ Some girls pass blood from nose, ears or anus instead of from their genitals which is a grave symptom (which is termed as 'Vicarious Menstruation') and should be treated by a doctor at the earliest. In certain cases, surgical interference may be the only alternative, especially when medicines fail to yield desired results.
- ☞ Certain girls suffer psychic upsets that may adversely affect flow of blood—it could either be scanty or profuse, depending on health condition of the girl.
- ☞ Anaemia is a common symptom with most of the girls who have drooping sensations, pant even on slightest labour, suffer from lumbago or indigestion, eructations, belching and flatulence. These symptoms can be easily managed.
- ☞ If menses cease, after having been established and running a full course, indicate that the girl is pregnant. Conception cannot be had without mating, hence there is always a danger of virgin girls becoming 'Virgin mothers' which, in our society, is an unchaste. So, the girls, high rate of sexual urge during or after cessation of monthly menses, an unethical event, should be guided to control their passions, by diverting their attention to other aspects.

SEX LIFE—PREMARITAL AGE

Fear of social sanctions and resultant social boycott is stiff rampant in our psyche. Sex, without marriage, is considered both a sin and crime. If any act is performed under fear psychosis, no pleasure can possibly be derived. Those people who indulge in premarital sex are not treated kindly in our society and have to face the wrath of society. No doubt , there are still a few neo-rich-families where sex, without marriage, is not considered an act that should raise eye-brows, though the element of admission and openness is still missing, and that may possibly be the reason as to why incest is still considered a religious and social crime.

Metrorrhagia and Menstrual Colic

Metrorrhagia

This disease is often confused with Menorrhagia—only common factor being profuse bleeding. In the case of metrorrhagia bleeding occurs during inter-menstrual periods when menses are not expected. That is, in this case bleeding occurs independent of menstruation gets extended or may even occur between interspace of two menstrual periods, but blood discharge is a morbid discharge.

Exciting Causes

Bleeding (at irregular interval) is quite common at the first menstrual period or at the time of menopause but contributory and exciting causes can be spelled as mentioned hereunder :

(1) Abuse of spirits, drugs, coffee, strong spices, tea, cocoa, etc.

(2) Women who have borne many children and that, too frequently.

(3) Standing erect for a long time, excessive walking (at a stretch); riding on horse-back, undertaking long journeys.

(4) Tightening and compressing the body by too tight

clothes, abdominal or other corsets.

(5) Exciting sex organs by, reading hotty and lascivious novels, prone magazines and watching porno photographs, pictures and movies, lascivious thoughts, exciting genitals by artificial devices.

(6) Use of abortive means.

(7) Excessive sexual intercourse and high frequency of indulgence.

(8) Those ladies who reside near sea-levels are more prone to this disorder.

(9) Sudden emotions like sudden shock, fear, intense joy, loss of some loved one.

Other causes of metrorrhagia

☞ Consequences of sneezing, coughing vomiting, non-stop hiccups.

☞ Moles or hydatid in the uterus, carcinomas, ulceration, polypi.

☞ Intestinal worms, inflammatory or gastric irritations that may trigger haemorrhage from the uterus.

☞ Forcible rape or excessive and prolonged intercourse.

☞ Violent exercise, like dancing, running, jumping, violent commotion of whole body.

☞ Displacement of womb.

☞ Cauterization of cervix (neck of womb).

☞ Irritating or warm injections in the vagina.

Symptoms

☞ Swelling of the breasts due to some infection or nursing of infants.

☞ Malaise and general weakness of body.

☞ Congestion towards the uterus.

☞ Constipation.

☞ Tension in the hypochondria, with heat, heaviness and pain in hytocawtric or sacral region.

- ☞ Cold extremities, face pale, general lassitude.
- ☞ Stertorous or laboured (embarassed) breathing or simple panting.
- ☞ Violent headache, especially in occipits.
- ☞ Itching of the parts and heat.
- ☞ Black rings around the eyes which are sunken.
- ☞ Oedema of the feet and legs, etc.

As a general rule, the more profuse and copious the flow, the less the duration and vice versa. In young girls, at the pubescene age, the discharge lasts for a few days and is followed by swelling and heat in the vulva and vagina, paleness of face, debility, rings around eyes, lassitude in the limbs and flabbiness of flesh. The discharge stops after a few days. During menopause, metrorrhagia lasts comparatively for a longer period and flow is generally profuse but stops after a few days, but resumes after an interval of 2-3 days. But in chronicity of disease, it may last for several years when blood discharged (quantity of blood passed) is not copious but most of the ladies may suffer from leucorrhoea, also alongside.

As for the appearance of blood, it is in clots due to accumulation of blood in the vagina. Active form of malady is often preceded by symptoms of local or general reaction. It runs a rapid course, its victims being stout and robust women, often passing coagulable blood. Passive form is always a chronic form. In passive metrorrhagia, position takes a turn-about when only lymphatic ladies fall a prey, there blood being impoverished and watery. In any case, sudden and profuse metrorrhagia, is very dangerous and, if not controlled in time, may terminate fatally. If there are ulcers, polypi or moles or cancer of the uterus, bleeding is difficult to control because the same cannot be controlled unless the underlying cause has been first deduced and then treated.

Menstrual Colic

When we refer to dysmenorrhoea, we imply painful menstruation and pain may precede (which often it does) a scant flow but subsidises as soon as flow becomes normal. Pain generally resembles a labour-like pain, when some young girls have been seen to faint even, under the stress and severity of attack. In certain ladies, it is utilised as an excuse (though rare) to take leave from domestic rut and routine. But, whenever a lady says she has menstrual pain, there is hardly any reason to suspect and, thus, deny her rest and treatment.

It 'is repeated that colic, during menstrual period, is quite natural though, degree, intensity and duration of pain often vary, depending on health status of a lady. During puberty, irregular menstruation, scanty and vicarious flow is quite common and thus, it should be taken as a normal and natural consequence. But, if the pain is persistent, severe and unbearable and affects normal daily work, then the same should he treated forthwith.

In anaemia, ladies menstrual flow is quite irregular and scanty. In such cases, attention should be directed to improving general health. When health has improved, severity and duration will eliminate. In order to raise Hb count in the blood, one should try to depend on natural foods (as already detailed earlier), instead of taking recourse to tonics. Aim should be to raise the level of resistance by supportive measures.

Abdominal colic and menstrual colic need to be deduced. In the former, there is constant gurgling and rumbling, and there is a feeling as if wind has here stuck up. Relief is felt when wind gets discharged but, in the latter type its seat seems to be uterus. It is either inflammatory or nervous in character which often resembles a labour pain and surfaces only at interval but is never constant. Pain is felt primarily in hips, loins, lower abdomen or/ and lower limbs. It often precedes menstrual flow but subsides as soon as normal flow is restored. In some cases, it may appear after the menstrual course has already started. Not only these but there are other causes that trigger colic of this variety but, then each case has its own history as to onset, progress and decline, which factors need to be investigated.

Causes of Menstrual Colic

- General ill-health, poor diet, anaemia.
- Exposure to cold or damp conditions.
- Retarted, interrupted or irregular menstrual flow.
- Errors and indiscretions in living mode.
- Imprudent use of drugs during menstrual flow.
- Some intractable disease.

General Symptoms

- Uneasiness and sense of well-being lost.
- Headache with or without constipation.
- Pain in lower abdomen and lower limbs.
- Irregular flow with pain.
- Pain in' hips, back, pubic area and feeling of general soreness.
- Lethargy and disinclination to perform even daily chores.
- Swelling of breasts and feet

Treatment

- Tab. Spomoproxivom when required or seek gynaecologist opinion.
- Hot formentation of the lower abdomen may be helpful.
- Avoid weight lifting, spicy-oily food.

Menopause or Critical Age

If puberty stage is a waterloo of adolescent girls, menopause is the waterloo of women in the middle period of their life (i.e. 45-50 years). There are three stages of menstruation viz.

1. Onset stage
2. Progressive stage
3. Terminal (final) stage

If a girt starts menstruating, say at the 15th years, she should generally reach menopause at or around the 45th year. It means a lady menstruates for about 28-35 years, starting from first menstruation and ending up in menopause. If the said criterion is disturbed, which often does is hardly any cause for anxiety or any treatment unless symptoms of grave nature surface and medical aid is called for. It is necessary to point out that total period of menstrual years varies from lady to lady. If menses have started earlier, one shouldn't assume that cessation will also take place on time or vice versa. Remember that :

☞ Onset of menses is a natural sequence and there is nothing unusual or unnatural about the same.

☞ Age in each lady may differ as to onset of menses and cessation of menses.

☞ Normal menstrual cycle is disturbed by pregnancy, free sexual indulgence, poor health, poor quality of blood, general ill-health, some chronic infective disease, habitual abortions, malnutrition, mental disturbances, uncongenial environs etc.

- Quantity of blood passed may be scanty, interrupted, profuse, intermittently slow and fast, with variable appearance in blood colour.
- Menses may be smooth and without any hassles, may be painful or debilitating,
- There may be episodes of vicarious menstruation.
- Mental status of a lady will favourably or adversely affect onset, course and termination of menstrual periods.
- Any physical problem, howsoever minor or negligible, must be treated by a physician.
- Finally, a lady whose menstruation process is normal/ regular is not likely to encounter any serious physical problem.

Some conspicuous points to be remembered

- Headache and backache; pain in cervical portion.
- General age, at which menopause should take place, ranges between 40 and 50 years of age, but normally in 45 and 46 years. But, it may occur earlier in warm climates and later in cold climates as a general rule; though exceptions can still be found to exist.
- Time of menopause is not, at all, dependant on upon retorted/delayed or earlier onset of first menstruation. A woman, who gives birth to more children, will have a comparative longer and prolonged menstrual periods until menses finally cease entirely.
- In most of the cases, many women do not even ever experience any untoward local disorder or any alarming symptoms whereas, for others, it may be one of the most critical periods in their life.
- Periods may return after 7-10-15-20 days, of every week, or after every 2-3 weeks or even 2-3-4-6 months. Timing, quantity of menstrual blood may be irregular.

- In nervous and plethoric ladies, there is onset of dangerous and alarming bleeding, especially in those who have indulged in sexual excesses.
- In certain women bleeding may also be accompanied by acrid, copious, foul-smelling, yellowish or whitish leucorrhoeal flow which may continue even after menstrual discharge has completely ceased.

Concomitant symptoms incidental to main disease

- Congestion of the head and haemoptysis (bloody urine, piles, nasal bleeding, and other vicarious bleedings).
- Vomiting, diarrhoea, weakness of stomach and other digestive problems.
- Profuse sweating and/or consumption.
- Rheumatic attacks on thighs, shoulders, swelling of joints etc. General soreness (feeling of) all over the body when even a slightest touch aggravates pain/ ache.
- Nymphomania, attacks of hysteria, other nervous disorders, hypochondria, agitated mood and behaviour, getting easily excited or nervous even on minor points and hypochondriacs.
- Skin eruptions (such as letters at the organs of generation, itching and pruritis; Acne erysapelas, rough skin etc.)
- Ulcers, polypi, carcinoma of the uterus and breast (or either of the organs) may prove even fatal at times, but not in cases of all women.
- Pains on sides of waist, uterine cramps, colic, feeling of weight in lower abdomen, pubes, loins.
- Severe or even incapacitating backache.
- Swelling of abdomen, constipation, or else loose and debilitating motions, often resulting in dehydration.

Treatment

If no untoward symptom surfaces, there is hardly any need to resort to any medicine but when some alarming situation has appeared, the concerned disease must be treated forthwith. In certain cases, concomitant symptoms are more serious than menopause itself. Certain symptomatic symptoms are quite natural and, thus, incidental to menopause. Use the medicines recommended under 'Amenorhoea, giving priority to Bryonia, Cocculus, Ignatia, Sabina, Sepia, Sulphur. Also reference may be made to medicines prescribed under cancer of womb, 'diseases of breasts', 'Metrorrhagia', 'Leucorrhoea', in addition to 'Amenorrhoea.'

Free flow of genital bleeding should not be interfered with, unless life itself is threatened. In some ladies, most of the disorders hardly surface and also that they are unaware of the organic changes that occur so gradually and slowly - almost being unnoticed.

Auxiliary Measures

Such measures are more important, for all the ladies who suffer from menopause. Menopause should be taken as a normal development, without getting emotionally and physically charged up. Avoid taking any medicine for every little distress, instead allow nature to play its part effectively. Complications can be minimised, if not totally eliminated, by resorting to following measures, such as :

(i) Take simple and proper diet that should be easily digestible, consisting nourishing and plain food items which must not be stimulating or heated.

(ii) Avoid tea coffee, cocoa, strong spices, alcohol, domestic drugs and formulations, deductions or medicines based merely on a hearsay or related benefits to some one else.

(iii) Avoid two extremes in respect of physical exercise—complete sedentary life or excessive exercises—pushed beyond the point of sustenance and tolerance.

(iv) Take regular and sustainable exercise in open and fresh air but make sure any exercise undertaken doesn't cause more flow of blood;

(v) Avoid living in over-heated or windy apartments and your own dress should also suffice to meet the demands of local climate. You will simply be inviting trouble if you wear such dress, as is against thermic levels.

(vi) Above all, remain accommodative, cheerful and happy go-lucky and learn to laugh away problems of daily life.

(vii) Take reasonable rest when body is tired, but never take rest when it is not required.

(viii) Desist from coition during entire period of menopause, as it may prove detrimentally injurious to both husband and wife. It would be still better if the lady is afforded freedom from coition, at least for 10-15 days, after menses have stopped finally.

Try following homoeopathic remedies as per symptoms noted against each.

Lachesis-6 : It is a chief medicine when there is sweating aggravation after waking, sensation (occasional) of flushes of heat.

If lachesis fails to give any relief, try Nit.3 or Sanguinaria3x when nervous symptoms supervene.

Anemia in Ladies

Anaemia literally means pallor or paleness of body which is accompanied by reduction in the quantity of hemoglobinan oxygen-carrying pigment- in the blood. In our country lack of good nutritional diet, poor living, ignorance about health-care rules, absence of personal hygiene, frequent child-bearing, mental and physical strain, cares and worries of so-called modem life, etc. are the general factors.

Symptoms of Anaemia

(i) Poor resistance to infections and infective diseases.
(ii) Excessive fatigue and tiredness, even on slightest attempt to labour.
(iii) Breathlessness on exertion (Effort-onset dyspnoea).
(iv) Disinclination to perform even daily chores.
(v) Pallor of face or general paleness of body.
(vi) Vertigo, poor eye-sight, palpitation.
(vii) Neuropathic symptoms, cloudiness of intellectual process, instant (partial) memory failure.
(viii) Vague muscle and body aches, dependant upon duration rapidity and intensity of iron-deficient-anaemia.
(ix) Lactation and lack of milk in breasts due to poor dietary standard.

Causes of Anaemia

(i) Iron-deficiency in pregnant, lactating mothers.
(ii) Unhealthy environs, poor diet but strenuous workload which the frail body is unable to bear and sustain.
(iii) Deficiency due to chronic blood loss, as in the case of menstrual bleeding, during abortion or child delivery, accident.
(iv) Poor and subnormal performance of digestive system, resulting in poor digestion.
(v) Premature babies.
(vi) Non-absorption of iron.
(vii) Some chronic and serious ailment.
(viii) Pernicious anaemia, when life itself is in danger.

Kinds of Anaemia

Hemorragic anaemia : Due to excessive bleeding.

Iron-deficiency anaemia : Due to lack of iron.

Hemolytic anaemia : Caused by increased destruction of red blood cells and triggered by toxic chemicals, parasites (particularly of malaria), thalasemia.

Pernicious anaemia : That which kills a person.

Gradually progressive anaemia : There is no sudden onset of anaemia due to some latent cause which is almost untraceable or else the cause is too obscure to be pin-pointed. This condition is opposite to sudden bleedings caused by excessive menstrual flow or from abortion or operation—either in the state of pregnancy or otherwise. Essential anaemia is more alarming than the anaernia (primary) where contributor cause has been deduced which is easy to cure.

Treatment

Take plenty of spinach, beet, tomato, sugarcane juice, pomegranates, milk and milk products in diet. Plenty of whole milk, cream, milk mixed with sugar-cane juice, tomato + beet

+ carrot juice, juice or cooked vegetable of spinach are capable of providing much needed iron to the body through natural foods. Mango juice, plain or mixed, with milk or raisins boiled with milk are excellent sources of natural iron. Grapes or grape juice can also be taken without being blended with any other drink.

Ferrum Phos 3x (4 Tabs 4 times daily) should be continuously taken for 2-3 months or till situation improves. Alfalfa tonic (10-15 ml) before principle meals daily will push up haemoglobin in the blood, in addition to improving appetite and digestion as a whole in general. Mother tincture of Alfalfa, (which is chief constituent of Alfalfa tonic, (in 5-10 drop doses—thrice daily-before meals) will show better and quicker results but it has also to be continued for 1-2 months or until anaemia disappears.

In Allopathy, iron preparations, in the form of tablets, syrups and injections are available which can be used with advantage according to need but a doctor's advice and supervision is essential so as to rule out chances of any reaction.

In Ayurveda, *Lauhasava* or *Lohitarishta* (20-25 ml) may be taken after meals or *Lauha Bhasma* with juice of Punarnava may be taken after meals daily.

Leucorrhoea—A Very Common Problem

It is generally called a 'white discharge' or simply 'the whites'. In reality, leucorrhoea is a state where there is catarrhal discharge from the Vagina's mucous membranes. This is the most agonising disorder for the females and distorts their health. It may last a lifetime or prolong for sometime and then abate or may appear as and when her health is in poor state.

Leucorrheal Flow

- The discharge is often white, like white portion of an egg or milk-colour, or else it may be off white, yellow, reddish or pinkish, green or light blue. But in most of the cases, it is odourless and white.
- Flow may stiffen the linen or simply leave back a trace of white powder or scales.
- It may excoriate vulva and thighs and the itching caused is sometime too intense and so much that blood oozes out from the site itched.
- Consistency of discharge varies from water to consistency of cream, milk, viscous fluid or even albuminous.
- In most cases discharge emanates from the uterine cavity or vagina. In catarrhal or idiopathic variety

of leucorrhea, the discharge is in mild and liquid form but does not excoriate or irritate the parts. But, when it is dependant inflammation organic lesions of uterus or its appendages the discharge becomes fetid, corrosive, acrid, brownish or green.

- The discharge from the uterus is often from uterine cavity, more albuminous, thick, viscid, flocculant, and has an allkaline reaction, whereas vaginal discharge is always acidic, thin, white, creamy and milky.
- Leucorrhoeal discharge is more profuse and copious at the time of menses than at any other time but in some ladies, it continuously goes on, though quantity of discharge varies.
- In certain ladies, leucorrhoeal discharge sets in even 8-10 days before anticipated period of menses and stops as soon as menses appear but, in others, it may start when menses are over.
- In some ladies leucorrhoea shows its presence instead of menses.
- General health of the lady is not affected if the leucorrhoeal discharge lasts for a short period, though there may be present general debility.
- If the discharge is copious and continues for a much longer period, there could be heaviness in the .epigastrium and pain. There is also capricious hunger, nausea and vomiting, fainting spells, desire for those things which have no relation to the malady; digestion is difficult and slow; vertigo, headache; slow motion and general lethargy, pain particularly in shoulder blades and generally in all the limbs; face is pale, livid, skin is discoloured and dull.
- When the leucorrhoeal discharge continues for a fairly long period, the patient feels exhausted even on any attempt to slight exertion. She grows weak and then, palpitation and breathlessness, dull and vacant looks, margin of eyes surrounded by black rings, all intellectual faculties are weakened and face is bloated.

Causes of Leucorrhoea

(1) Affects mostly nervous, lymphatic, feeble, cathetic ladies who have fair complexion, pale skin and soft skin.

(2) No age is immune from its attack—it can occur anytime between 15-45, though even children at the fairly much younger age (say 8-10) have been the sufferers.

(3) Ladies who migrate from one place to another, i.e. from villages to cities; live in recently built dwellings, more particularly when houses are situated in deep and narrow valleys, damp and marshy places. In short, it is most common in damp and cold regions.

(4) There is hardly any endemic leucorrhoea, though undoubtedly some regional foods are deficient in certain elements which trigger episode of leucorrhoea.

(5) Exposure to cold and insufficient exposure of shoulders and neck to cold air, abuse of warm baths and warm injections.

(6) Depression, self modification, brooding, sudden shocking news or death, loss etc.

(7) Hereditary factor, though not very prominent, cannot be ignored or overlooked.

(8) Eating oysters crabs, fish, acid fruits, hard water, beer, cider, too much use of tea, coffee, purgatives.

(9) Self-vice or onanism, too much indulgence in sex act, nymphomania, presence of foreign bodies within vagina (like pessaries, sponges etc.)

(10) Menstrual irregularities, uterine displacements, pregnancy, miscarriage, worms in intestines, confinement, easy-going life style, pulmonary pthisis, chronic constipation.

(11) Piles, diarrhoea, suppression of sweat, milky secretion, bronchial expectoration, vomiting, cold in the head.

(12) Cancers and ulcerations, local inflammation, engorgement of cervix (neck of the uterus).

(13) Presence of gonorrhoea, resulting in inflammation, chancres, other growths.

Leucorrhoea of recent origin isn't, at all, difficult to cure but, when in chronic form, treatment is not only difficult but much tedious also, as one has to cure not only leucorrhoea but also other concomitant symptoms., Complications accompanying this disease are most difficult to cure than the main disease itself.

Auxillary Treatment

- A proper hygiene and cleanliness should be mentioned—of undergarments and sex organs, both.
- Avoid sour preparations, spicy-oily food.
- Consult a gynaecologist for proper diagnosis of leucorrhoea and then only start treatment.

Hysteria and Hysteralgia

Hysteria is a kind of neurosis. Prof. Freud, a reputed psycho-analyst, was of the view that this disease arises as a result of frustrated libidenous impulses. It is believed to occur in chronic virgins mostly who have been denied the pleasure of sexual union and also that when they have already passed their marriage age.

Hysteria is occasioned by following factors :

- Suppressed sexual desire, or
- Sudden withdrawal from sex act, after having indulged in frequently prior to attack.
- Emotional instability.
- Repression (of sexual desire).
- Changes in thinking or thinking disorders.
- Long drawn virginity.
- Personality disorders.
- Shallowness and instability of feelings.
- Young married girls whose husbands die soon after marriage and who are, then, forced to lead a virgin's life.

Hysteria is an abnormal mental condition that produces morbid changes in various functions of the body. Some authorities term it merely a state of mind, whereas others regard it simply a disease. There may, or may not be, any changes in structures of the nerves which we generally fail to discover. From epilepsy viewpoint, hysteria is closely related to chorea or epilepsy, and predisposition is nurtured by many improper mode of living. In many cases, yielding to the desires of an easy or sensual nature, during childhood, in particular, is the main contributory cause, though heredity is most frequently the first cause and contagion is the second cause.

Though women, between the age of 15-30, are more prone to hysterical attacks, yet men also are the victims. Profound mental or moral emotions, sudden success or reverses in life or business, any type of excitement or worry; late onset of puberty or delayed menses and cessation of menses could also be the probable causes.

Virgin pregnancy is also a cause of hysteria, or else first gestation of the neurotic married one (girl or lady). Fear, joy, sorrow, disgust, religious excitement are other exciting causes. Prof Freud propounded the theory that 'hysteria is always due to physical or psychic trauma and in most of the cases is sexual.

Symptoms

- ☞ Restlessness and irritability.
- ☞ Desire for sympathy and craving for notoriety.
- ☞ Discontentment and depression or exaltation.
- ☞ Abnormal desires and aversions
- ☞ Gastric disturbances, vomiting, nausea.
- ☞ Cursing or praying (or even alternatively) laughing and crying.
- ☞ Shrieking, screaming, beating of chest, or tearing of the clothes.
- ☞ Occasional involuntary stools and passing large quantity of urine.
- ☞ Fairly prolonged period(s) of unconsciousness.
- ☞ Presence of 'Aura' (Premonition or feeling of impending hysterical fits.
- ☞ Points and Centres of 'aura' may pertain to testicle, ovary (in case of males and females respectively), cerebral or spinal or cutaneous nerve centre.

- All forms of convulsions and convulsive movements, combination of muscles or a single muscle may be involved.
- In most of the cases complete consciousness is not lost but convulsive movements are followed by light sleep in the mild form.
- Bradycardia (slow pulse) or tachycardia (rapid pulse).
- Total absence of urine or excessive passage of urine.
- Foul odour is present in the majority of cases.

Auxiliary Treatment

- Do not resort to long periods of rest and sleep.
- Avoid undue worry, excitement.
- Examine carefully all the excretory organs.
- Children of neurotic persons should be looked after properly and served with proper food, induced for taking outdoor exercises.
- No protective treatment or extra caution is required, as such patients injure themselves very rarely.
- Let alone the patient.
- Children, at the age of puberty, need extra and special attention with regard to their pattern of nourishment, sleep, and they must be given freedom from excitement. Do not create any psychic phobia for the patient and never paint a morosed and distressing picture as to her malady.
- Give sympathetic and parental care to the children and, for this, teachers and parents need to join hands for co-operation.

Sterility/Infirtility/Frigidity

STERILITY

The term 'sterility' means inability to have (or conceive) children but applies equally to men also who are unable to impregnate a woman in order to enable her to conceive. But the term is applied frequently in case of women only. Sterility may be caused by following factors —

- Removal of ovaries/fallopian tubes.
- Non-production of ovum.
- Sexual unresponsiveness.
- Deranged position of uterus.
- Some ailments of chronic nature.
- Some hormonal disturbance.
- Frequent abortions.
- Consequence of some accident, etc.

Due to advances made in surgical spheres, sterility can be removed and cured if basic cause pertains to some organic defect. In most of the cases, it is the man who is at fault and not the woman. No doubt, atrophy of fallopian tube is still an unresolved problem but other organic defects can be successfully encountered. An adept gynaecologist can easily deduce the cause of sterility and remove the cause by surgical or other means, but timely detection and proper treatment is of paramount importance; hence corrective and curative measures must not be delayed.

Certain ladies nurture innate hatred towards male sex, due to which factor they fail to reach orgasm, thereby impeding the process of onset of pregnancy. Inbuilt inhibitions, fear psychosis, like enormous length of male penis, imagined pain during coitus, resulting in spasms, fits or pains or even avoidance of coitus are the other factors that could render a woman sterile. The husband should try to set at rest all the fears, inhibitions and imagined problems by sustained persuasion, love, affection, sympathy and reassurance. He should not behave like a stud, but a sympathetic, considerate and caring husband. Rest of the problems can be taken care of by the doctor. If there is a close rapport between both the partners, most of the problems related to sterility can be solved.

INFERTILITY

Here, inability to impregnate is the main cause and in over 90% cases, it is the husband (man) who is at fault. Truly speaking the two terms, viz sterility and infertility in a sense, are two sides of the coin, but cause of malady lies with the husband who has weak sperms which are not potent enough to cause conception. In most of the cases, woman is found to be quite fertile to bear a child by conceiving but is failed, quite often, by her male partner who either does not or cannot reach orgasm or suffers from premature ejaculation in which case the poor lady is left in the lurch. Such a situation causes family problems, feuds between husband and wife, psychic upsets and mental agitation (in women) and a sense of self-condemnation and inferiority (in the males). I have myself seen many family lives shattered due to sexual incompetence of men who either suffer from some psychological complex, sense of shame or have some organic or psychic problem as the underlying causes.

A sensible wife should reassure her husband in this regard and never let him feel demeaned or slighted. She should co-operate with him and help him in maintaining his self-confidence. It is absolutely an imprudent and immature approach to blame each other, instead of having mutual understanding. Healthy looking men are not necessarily potent men. Actually physical appearance and physical structure have nothing to do with virility and sexual performance or competence of a male.

Irrespective of sex, if either of the partners had indulged in self-vice or onanism in adolescence or until they were married or had premarital sexual relations, had been suffering from some venereal disease or indulged in homosexual or heterosexual (free) love, are liable to suffer from syndrome of infertility. All venereal diseases are now fully curable, organic problems can be coached by medicines, operations or psychological treatment.

FRIGIDITY

'Frigidity' implies sexual unresponsiveness towards sex and, here, either of the partners can be at fault but a lady partner is often made the scapegoat. Women of frigid nature are called 'Cold' women who do not respond to sexual advances of men, and end up as passive non-performers during intercourse. Those who get easily excited and quickly submit to sex are called 'hot' women. Similarly men can also be categorised under the said divisions. Here, the point, under discussion, is sexual unresponsiveness when either of the partners fails to measure up to the sexually heightened, voluptuous sprees and advances of the other partner . The restatement of one-sided sexual excitement is premature ejaculation, thus leaving the other partner mid-way to reel under pangs of instigated sex pleasure.

It is necessary to point out that desire to have sex is a paramount factor and if there is no desire in both the partners, coition is merely a formality or an obligation or compulsion—it is only a meeting of bodies but not of minds. For a successful and satiating sex, meeting of body and mind is of utmost necessity. Ejaculation is no guarantee for a satisfactory sex nor can it be termed as 'equal indulgence.'

Sex is not intended to be performed in isolation of body

and mind. You can satisfy your sex appetite by indulging in other means also, but you won't say 'you have enjoyed it fully'. There is room for partial or casual enjoyment—it is either complete enjoyment or none at all. One-sided sex is a matter of sheer discharging an imposed (social) obligation in respect of your partner or your own self.

There could be following gradational stages of frigidity, viz. :

1. The woman may show or actually be indifferent towards intercourse (sexual) and may indulge and participate in it simply as a part of her duty towards her husband. In such a situation, she neither abhors nor dislikes option but, all the same, she never enjoys it.
2. The woman does not reach her orgasm, even thought she enjoys it. There is a feeling that her participation is quite normal and also that woman's performance is also identical so far as intensity and pleasure are concerned.
3. She may nurture a positive repugnance for sexual intercourse but her body 'freezes' even on an idea having a coitus. She is merely a passive participant.
4. Fear coitus, especially in young ladies who nurture baseless feelings and suffer from most or anyone the following symptomatic factors, viz :

Any physical problem like headache, pain in breasts and nipples, small breasts, aching in body, palpitation, giddiness, depression, hystirical fits on insertion of male penis, abnormal length and thickness of penis, pain on penile insertion, crying, trembling, nervosity, discharges from vagina, colliquative (debilitating) sweating, etc.

Some women are scared of when a surgeon probes fingers into her vagina. Even the idea of male penerating his penis into her vagina may send shivers down her spine, cause spasms in vagina.

In either case, it is the fear of penetration that triggers frigidity syndrome.

A few ladies remain cool to sexual intercourse because

they would hate to bear a child lest their beauty is marred or their figure is spoiled. Such ladies avoid their husbands and pretend one excuse or the other in order to avoid coitus. This, in fact, is not directly related to any kind of frigidity but is merely an excuse to abstain from sex. These ladies often complain of pain in body, skin rash, itching of vulva, headache, back pain, etc., so that their husbands may not compel them to have an intercourse. Going to sleep or pretending sleepiness is a common excuse of such reluctant ladies. In fact, such excuses ate employed as 'escape routes' to avoid or get rid of coitus.

Frigidity also stems from following contributory factors, apart from the ones already indicated above :

☞ Inhuman and bestial behaviour of male members with mothers, sisters and also discriminatory treatment.

☞ Organic incompetence.

☞ Inbuilt psycho-phobia about intercourse, that it is a filthy, derogatory human instict that underscores, demeans and degrades a woman's status and that woman is treated merely as a sex-tool.

☞ Lack of proper sex knowledge. She has no idea of male and female sex organs and the individual utility and functions of each organ.

☞ Fear of rupture of hymen or if the same has already been ruptured in premarital period, she is suspicious that her husband may suspect her virginity.

☞ Even ignorance of male, in respect of sexual posture and foreplay, drive a woman away from sexual indulgence. Here, the male member should play his role to introduce variety into coital postures and foreplay.

☞ In crowded families and that too when there is no place for privacy in a joint family, women generally abhor and avoid sex. The problem is more grave in tradition bound families where husband-wife cannot eat together nor go out for a walk nor talk to each other. Such indirectly imposed restrictions inhibit a woman's sexual urges, resulting in her frigidity.

Pregnancy

Marriage and It's Benefits

Marriage is a pious institution that binds two known/ unknown persons of both sexes into a wedlock. Initiation and perpetuation of progeny is considered a sacred duty of all couples (married, of course). Sex during marital life is simply an acclaimed and established way and there is no ground for any inhibitions and age-old taboos. After all there is, and ought to be, no secret between husband and wife. Conjugal love is best expression of sex-love, as no sense of guilt of or remorse is involved here.

Benefits of Marital Sex

- It is free from taboos and inhibitions, as also from fear and reservations.
- It is not a union of two bodies only but also of two minds and souls and the opportunity is utilised, quite often, to bring both the partners to come nearer and understand each other well.
- It is a positive approach to ease physical fatigue and mental stress. It has been often observed that what cannot be achieved through medicinal treatment can be easily attained within a few minutes of conjugal love.
- Emotional involvement is the basic factor that creates an atmosphere of mutual understanding.

- ☞ It lays foundation of a happy married life and eases charged up sentiments.
- ☞ It is a complete exercise in itself as there is no organ of the body whose functionality is not improved upon. Endocrine glands function properly, thus activating sex urge, sexual organs and pleasure.
- ☞ Sex helps to break mental, emotive and physical barriers and rips apart all the misgivings.

Prohibitive Factors

1. Ignorance about sex organs of both sexes.
2. Imprints of torture by men of (ladies in) infancy, adolescence and young age.
3. Disinformation and lack of properly guided knowledge as to sex act and pleasures emanating therefrom.
4. Family history, culture and relations between both the parents.
5. Fear psychosis.
6. Revulsion due to rough handling by the dominant male partner.
7. Inconvenient sex postures that cause pain, agony and revulsion towards sex act.
8. 'Cold ladies', indifferent behaviour.
9. Some psychic or/and physical problem.
10. (Pseudo) superiority complex about her better looking form, official status, financial status and dominant behaviour and arrogant temperament.
11. Endocrine gland disorders and chronic debilitating diseases.
12. Fear of pregnancy, pregnancy—related problems, losing her 'shape'.

There could be, and are, many other problems that may inhibit a married lady to despise sex. In our traditional Indian homes lack of privacy is also another major factor that drives the married couples away from sex act and sex enjoyment and the problem is more grievous in a joint-family. Those men and women who had taste of pre-marital sex generally do not reconcile mentally to a new partner's sex urge. In feudal families, extra-marital relations are not considered unsoical, unethical but a symbol of feudal glory, when the wife is treated as one among other slaves and, thus, does not enjoy status of a wife. Development of sex relations between married ladies and unmarried youngmen, servants is a common sight or even husband's friends also seize the opportunity to enjoy sex with sex-starved ladies.

Sex related disorders (Due to dissatisfied sex)

- Agitated and withdrawn behaviour
- Menstrual disorders
- Communicable diseases
- Hysteria, Epilepsy, Leucorrhoea
- Neurasthenia, nervous debility, loss or lack of sleep or disturbed sleep pattern.
- Somnabulance (sleep walking)
- Hysterical fits or even comatose
- AIDS
- Urinary problems and venereal diseases
- Backache, lassitude, pains and aches (in general).

Tests Used in Pregnancy

Various tests and procedures are used in certain cases of pregnancy complications. Like all medical procedures, they offer advantages, but also carry risks. Therefore, they should be utilized only when medically indicated, not on a routine basis for your or your doctor's convenience or to satisfy your curiosity.

Among the more common tests used in pregnancy are:

- Ultrasound
- Foetal movement evoluation
- Hoemoglobin and general blood picture
- Blood group and Rh factor
- Thyroid profile
- Blood Sugar
- Tests related to sexually transmitted diseases

But let your doctor decide, which test is required for you.

Pregnancy and its Symptoms

How Conception Takes Place

As a general rule every woman passes blood from her vagina after a gap of 28 days and the bleeding lasts for about 4-5 days. Regular onset of menses and cessation are indicators to fine health of a woman. In some cases menses may start even a bit earlier or later than a gap of 28 days and may last for less or more than 4-5 days but, once the cycle gets established, there should be no disturbance as to the start and duration of monthly periods. Any deviation, except the marginal one, points to ill-health or some disease which should be quickly investigated, if menses are irregular, there are more than one bleedings or excessive or scanty bleedings, much pain, weakness, malaise, run-down condition, anaemia etc. Back pain and pain in pubic region are almost common symptoms to all the ladies.

It should be borne in mind that all intercourses do not and cannot result in conception. Ideal time for conception is believed to be after one week of menses and before one week of next menses. Life of eggs is said to 3-4 days at the most or 24 hours on the lower side. There are countless eggs which fertilise and travel via fallopian tubes to the uterus, but only one of such eggs is able to establish contact with the male sperm and rest of which are destroyed. If, however, the sperm fails to meet the ovum, no conception can take place. Another time for conception is most likely to take place within 3-4 days of end of the monthly menstrual period. If husband and wife conjugate during this period, there are brighter chances for the woman to conceive.

A lady should keep a chart of her menstrual cycles and know fully well when her monthly period has ended. If no menstruation takes place at the designated time after cohabitation, it is a sign of pregnancy. If there is presence of clear mucus at the neck of uterus and there is increase in flow of such mucus (which serves to help facilitate travel of ova from the cervix (neck of uterus), it is a clear sign that the lady's ovum is ready to establish contact with its male counterpart (that is sperm). So, discharge of clear mucus from the vagina during menses is a clear indication of presence of ova in the uterus. At the height of simultaneous orgasm and ejaculation, both the mating partners help in the process of conception—when male sperm meets the female ovum.

The Expected Date of Delivery (EDD)

The delivery is expected to take place nine months and seven days from the first day of the menstruation preceding the conception or the Last Menstrual Period (LMP). In simple words, the reckoning of the date of conception is the lady's last menstrual period. If the period began on the first January 1991, the expected date of delivery would be 8th October 1991. However there is no hard and fast rule about it. The date varies depending upon the conditions of the pregnant lady.

The Growth of the Baby in the Foetus

The lady's visit to the doctor at least once in a month in the initial stage and every fortnight in the final stages is necessary not only for ascertaining the condition of the expectant mother but also the growth of the baby in the uterus. How the baby develops in foetus in shown in the table given below.

Elapsed weeks from Last Menses	Average Height of the foetus (in cms.)	Average weight of foetus (In gms.)
8	About 0.23	About 1
12	" 6	" 14
16	" 12	" 108
20	" 16	" 316
24	" 21	" 630
28	" 25	" 1045
32	" 28	" 1680
36	" 32	" 2478
40	" 36	" 3250

Routine Medical Check up

The expectant mother should begin, after having consulted her family physician, to get herself registered in a reputed clinic/home/hospital—of course with the advice of her doctor and follow the directions given by her doctor. Then she should begin to visit the chosen establishment regularly and keep her doctor informed fully about the progress of her pregnancy, the state of her health and all details especially if she notices any departure from the normal expected pattern. It must be remembered that the more she cooperated with her physician the easier be the delivery.

Exercise

Together with the above mentioned precautions the lady should take adequate physical exercises suiting her body condition. If the development of the foetus is preceding normally and there are no physical reasons to the contrary, she should take routine exercises as are advisable in her condition. But she must always be careful that she doesn't overtire herself. In particular, she should perform exercises which tone up the muscles of the waist, the back and abdomen.

Rest and Sleep

Shakespeare was not wrong when he observed in one of his plays "Sleep the chief nourisher of the life's feast!" Sleep provides that rest to the body limbs without which they can't sustain themselves no matter what you eat. Good sleep is the indication that your body has assimilated the nourishment you have given to it for food. However, slight complication occurs in the pregnant women's case because they generally get tired more easily, especially in the first and last trimesters (three month periods of pregnancy). She should provide for sufficient rest in her daily routine. Normally it would be advisable for her to rest daily for eight hours at night and an least two hours in the day time. As the time for delivery draws near, she needs longer periods of rest. She should increase the daily periods of rest to at least 10 hours at night and at least four hours in the day time, making a total of 14 to 16 hours of rest in every 24 hours. The expectant mother must form the habit of sleeping with her feet resting at slightly higher levels than the rest of the body. On no account should she sleep with her knees bent, nor sit with legs folded under as in a kneeling position. Such positions are likely to obstruct the circulation of blood in the lower regions of the legs, causing those parts to smell.

Insomnia often troubles pregnant women. In general their tendency is to resort to taking sleeping pills. But such drugs may cause harm to a pregnant lady as well as to the baby inside her. In such cases advise of the physician should be sought.

Self-Cleaning and Clothing/foot wear etc.

Bathing regularly is a must because it itself is a mild but effective exercise. She should bath every day, scrubbing each part of the body well. Preferably a tub should be used for the baths. However, she should exercise great care while sitting down, standing up or moving in the bathroom so as to avoid slipping. Even a minor accident in this stage could have grave consequences. Taking bath with warm water is advisable The genitals should be cleaned thoroughly with warm water.

The expectant mothers should wear clothes that allow them to move freely, without any inconvenience whatsoever. Nowadays in vogue are the loose-fiting robes called ' maternity gown' which cover the body well and present a becoming experience, as they definitely cover up the bulge of the abdomen in their folds. The breasts ought to be supported by a well fitting brassier. She should stop wearing high healed footwear. Besides giving extra pressure to the torso they make it difficult to keep one's balance. Only flat-soled shoes or chappals must be worn . While walking she should always maintain a leisurely pace and should never rush for anything.

Precautions During Pregnancy

These precautions should be taken during pregnancy.

Exposure to Radiation of X-rays, etc.

It is a well established fact that X-rays are harmful to the foetus, especially in the embryonic stages. The expectant mother should never permit herself to be X-rayed, or take radiotherapy or any treatment which exposes her to harmful radiations. Such radiations may not give any adverse effect immediately but might cause deformity in the baby even after delivery. In case she needs to be X-rayed for some medical reason, she must seek her physician's advice.

Journeys

A pregnant woman should avoid any journey in which she is forced to sit unmoved for long hours. Barring a two-three hours car/bus/travel, she shouldn't undertake long journeys. Of course she can travel by train which allows free movement to the passengers. But avoid taking the upper birth. However, in the last stages she should not take any long journey by any mode of travel.

Smoking

Nicotine is a harmful substance for the pregnant ladies' body chemistry. The babies born to women who are given to smoking are generally smaller in size and lighter in weight. Their deliveries are generally not easy, and in a large number of cases, the pregnancies end in miscarriages. Even if pregnancies are successfully carried to term, the babies are generally found vulnerable to bacterial infections and respiratory diseases. The nicotine from the tobacco can find its way to the foetus, which would induce malformations of certain organs, or defects in the hearts of the babies. Such babies start having chest pains in the very first year of their lives. Smoking women often become victims of haemorrhages during pregnancy. Hence smoking should be shunned by the pregnant women if they want no trouble during pregnancy or even later.

Drinking Alcohol

Drinking alcoholic beverages is positively harmful to a pregnant woman. A baby developing in the womb of a woman who drinks may be defective in one way or the other. Defects of heart muscles, fingers, toes and even faces are commonly observed in such babies. The nose is flattened, the jaw lack their normal contours, the nervous system doesn't function well, and stammering or stuttering is likely to affect the speech of the child when it grows up. Even for the lady alcohol is injurious. In case the woman is addicted, she might take some light wines to satisfy her urge partially, that too after consulting her physician.

Sex During Pregnancy

Doctors generally opine that coitus need not be avoided till about 37th week of pregnancy. However, if there is a history of abortion then coitus ought to be avoided in the first four months. The husband must take care about choosing the posture for the sexual intercourse and see to it that the abdomen of the woman is not exerted pressure upon in any condition.

Drugs and Vaccines

During the first four months of pregnancy no vaccine should be administered unless the doctor advises under specific prescription. Normally tetanus vaccines are generally administered in the sixth, seventh and eight month of pregnancy. Once these injections have been taken during the first pregnancy, only one injection of tetanus vaccine suffices during subsequent pregnancies. Drugs of any kind are strictly prohibited during pregnancy unless recommended by the treating physician in some special conditions.

Place of Delivery

Now-a-days very rarely delivery is arranged at home, purely for the safety reasons. Generally Hospital/Nursing Homes/Private Clinics are preferred. However, with the going charges for delivery getting exorbitantly high, some still prefer to have delivery at home. In case delivery is arranged to take place at home, the confinement room should be airy and well lighted. The bed should be placed in such a way as to leave sufficient space for movement on all four sides. Unnecessary articles of furniture etc. should be removed from the room. The doctor, nurse or midwife finds it more convenient if the cot or bed is sufficiently high. All equipment and material necessary for the mother and baby as advised by the doctor should be kept ready and accessible, so that there is no occasion for rushing about looking for things at the crucial time.

General Precautions about Medication

The pregnant woman must always bear in her mind that she in now responsible for the life of two beings—she herself and her baby in the womb. Her eating, drinking and even taking patent medicines ought to be guided by this fact, for anything taken by a pregnant woman finds its way into the body of the baby within an hour. The limbs of the baby are in the process of formation during the first twelve weeks of pregnancy. Foreign substance like drugs introduced into the system during this part may disturb this process or development. Most, if not at all, congenital defects of the babies are traceable to the ingestion of excessive amounts of powerful toxic drugs. There are numerous instances on record of babies with malformed defects and various other deficiencies in development born to mothers who had been taking drugs like thalidomide (a sedative), androgens, synthetic progesterone and drugs for treatment of cancer, during the period of their pregnancies. That is precisely why it is desirable for the expectant mother to avoid taking any medicines, with the exception of vitamins, minerals or insulin. She shouldn't voluntarily resort to taking any drug unless recommended by the physician treating her.

There are certain special cases also. If the mother-to-be is a diabetic, the amount of sugar in her blood has to be controlled with the help of insulin, administered in right amount. Usually tablets, containing organic iron are also given to a pregnant woman to prevent anaemia. These tablets are usually formulated specifically for women in this condition and are, therefore, comparatively safe. Often other elements required in minor proportions, such as copper, managnese, magnesium and cobalt are included in the formulation of such tablets. Tablets of folic acid are also prescribed for the pregnant woman at her very first visit to the doctor, and she is usually required to take these tablets throughout the duration of her pregnancy. Calcium formulations are administered to relieve muscular pain. All these substances are enzymes and food supplements rather than drugs or medicines, and so are considered relatively safe. Acetaminophen is administered to pregnant woman in place of aspirin as an analgesic, but even this drug is not entirely harmless. It has a harmful effect on the liver and kidney and should be taken only if it becomes absolutely necessary. Immoderate quantities of drugs affecting nerves, such as barbiturates, amphetamines and opium preparations are dangerous for the baby, as they may impede growth, and even lead to a reduction in the weight of the baby. That is why a pregnant woman must not resort to any medicine in the hope of finding an immediate cure which is the prevalent tendency now-a-days. The expectant mother should exercise greater discretion and should accept only those medicines that are prescribed by her doctor.

Coping with the Physical Changes

As pregnancy advances the pregnant woman would find certain changes occurring in her body. The breasts begin to swell and harden. The areola round the nipples begins to darken, abdomen gets protruded and marks start quickly appearing on this region whenever it is scratched. In medical parlance, this condition is called Linca Alba.

These are natural and not abnormal changes that occur in a pregnant lady's body. Some of these symptoms occur because of high blood pressure which most of the pregnant ladies normally suffer from .

(i) High Blood Pressure - It is not a very common problem although some ladies do have high blood pressure during the second Trimester. However, high blood pressure problem with the ladies having a history of the trouble is definitely a matter of great concern. When the doctor comes across a pregnant woman with a history of high blood pressure he/she generally considers three possibilities.

(a) Pregnancy itself may have raised the blood pressure.

(b) She may be having undiagnosed-pre-existing-high blood pressure.

(c) Rise in blood pressure may have been caused by toxaemia of pregnancy—a condition in which there is salt and water retention, protein in the urine, and swelling of the ankles and fingers—all due to poisoning by bacteria. Toxaemia of pregnancy can endanger the mother's life and that of the unborn baby. It is best, in such cases, to move the pregnant mother to the hospital for treatment.

High blood pressure in pregnancy not caused due to toxaemia can be treated in much the same way as a non-pregnant woman suffering from it, but there are some differences. Detailed examinations, such as X-ray examination should be avoided until the baby is born. Doctors may prescribe as few drugs as possible, especially those which are known to be safe and the drugs which aim at weight reduction and salt restriction.

Ladies with a history of high blood pressure must inform the doctors as soon as conception takes place. Always remember, the more details you tell about yourself the easier it would be for the doctor to treat you. With modern treatment, even very severe cases of high blood pressure can be brought through pregnancy safely.

(ii) Early Fatigue- As hinted earlier, fatigue and lethargy are the commonest symptoms of the initial period of pregnancy. In fact, in the rural area of India where medical facility is not easily available, the old ladies would confirm pregnancy by these symptoms only. This is a nature's way to force the pregnant lady to relax and shun indulging in strenuous jobs. It is essential to relax for an hour after taking your bath and then at least for two hours after taking your meals. Many a time the pregnant lady's mother-in-law or other old ladies fail to realise that this fatigue or a slight loss of vitality cannot be made good by feeding the lady extra rich-ghee-filled-diet. For diet, howsoever rich it may be, cannot replace the efficacy of sleep. Hence sleep is essential to overcome this feeling of early fatigue. Another disadvantage of having very rich diet is its enhancing unwanted fat of the body. This accumulated fat is difficult to get rid of even in the post delivery period. That is the reason why in India of yesteryears the lady used to be fat but weak. Because the diet steeped in ghee and butter does not provide those extra vitamins, minerals and protein without which the vitality of the body cannot be enhanced.

It is after 18th week or so of conception that this feeling

of fatigue vanishes, only to return in the last month of pregnancy. This is the normal cycle of waxing and waning fatigue. However, if fatigue has been caused by mal-nutritious diet the doctor and the ladies of the household should pay more attentions to the pregnant lady's diet.

(iii) Cramps - Most of the pregnant ladies experience cramps at the onset of night. These cramps are the outcome of lack of calcium in the body. This can be easily controlled by increasing the intake of calcium in the body through diet and calcium tablets. The age old remedy—' The Banslochan' is also very useful to take out this trouble. Sometimes these cramps result due to varicose veins. These can be treated by the ' leg-lift' exercises given ahead. The lady should take precautions of not sitting in any position which requires hanging of the feet.

(iv) Pains In Hips and Waist - These are also the common complaints. Owing to the distention of the upper stomach due to pregnancy, extra pressure is put on the spinal chord which manifests itself in the form of pains in these parts. To ease this pressure on the spine the lady must learn how to carry her body in a fully balanced way which is elaborated in the exercises explained in separate chapter.

Another reason of these pains is somewhat ' loosening' of the tissues joining the pelvic region with the backbone. The hormone progesterone which is discharged in the large quantity is actually responsible for lossening of these tissue joints. But it is nature's way of facilitating the delivery of the child. Those ladies with heavier built feel it in a more pronounced way. The only way to redeem this trouble is to learn how to carry yourself in a more balanced way and to avoid hanging your feet.

Sometimes lack of calcium in the body also causes this pain. As we know a pregnant lady's body has also to procure calcium required to develop the child body. Hence this deficiency is natural. If their food doesn't supply calcium in adequate manner for long the lady herself becomes a patient of ' osteomalasia' which is a medical term for the weakening of the pelvic region. So the lady and those attending on her must ensure that she gets liberal amount of calcium through her diet and medication. This deficiency has to be taken care immediately because it might weaken the bones of the child also.

(v) Short of Breath - This is also a common problem during the last phase of pregnancy. Owing to the increase in the size of the embryo more pressure is exerted on the diaphragm causing this problem. Since the head of the child slides down a few weeks before delivery, the lady feels the temporary relief, otherwise, because of this problem she is advised to use a couple of pillows to breathe properly during her sleep. Lack of blood in the body also surfaces this problem. For making good this deficiency the lady must consume a lot of spinach, beet-roots, apples, besides having iron-rich tonics recommended by her doctor. If she practises pranayama regularly in the initial stages of pregnancy, she might not feel this problem as much as others feel.

(vi) Heart-burn- As hinted earlier , this problem has no concern with the heart. it is said heart-burn because near the heart-region a peculiar burning sensation is felt which is because of the acidity.

It can be taken care of by having edible alkaline substance like milk of magnesia, carbonic soda, unsalted salad piece like cucukmber in ample quantity etc. If the trouble persists with great acuteness the lady should have very balanced diet and should sleep with her head at proper height.

(vii) Tastelessness- Because of certain hormonal secretion, saliva production increases in great quantity.This is also one of the old tests to confirm pregnancy. This causes the pregnant ladies to
have special liking for chalk and other unusual things which do not even come in the edible category. The best way to fight this unusual longing is to make the lady have calcium rich things like its special tablets, the Banslochan etc.

(viii) Change of the colour of skin - As already explained, after 18 weeks the areola round the nipple begins to darken. It is less noticed in the fair complexioned ladies. Sometimes the darkness also spreads upto the breasts. These changes vanish after delivery but not completely. Application of special creams like the 'E-creams' helps remove them to certain extent. Sometimes a long-line appear below the navel also. The rings round the eyes also get darkened which automatically vanish after the delivery.

(ix) Stomach pain - As light pain is experienced in the 16-20th week of the pregnancy which is due to the pressure experienced by the lady owing to the increase in the size of the embryo. This is quite normal .In case the pain is of shooting type, the doctor ought to be immediately consulted.

(x) Swelling of the feet - This has also been explained and is caused by the veins getting rather vericose. Only when the feet continue to be swollen even after a full night's sleep that physician must be consulted.

(xi) Lack of Sleep- In the last trimester, lack of sleep is the common complaint. There could be several reasons for it, chief among them are the following :

(a) Repeated urge to urinate
(b) Due to the fast movement of the child inside the womb.
(c) A slight abnormal temperature of the body
(d) Short of breath and heart-burn complaints
(e) Cramps
(f) The nagging pain in the back or hip region

It is certainly not advisable to have sleeping pills or other kind of sedatives in the last trimester,. The lady should try to sleep with a peaceful mind. Washing hand and feet with lukewarm water and having hot milk before retiring for the day are some of the time tested formulae to induce sleep. In case the insomnia persists then the doctor should be consulted for having mild sedatives.

(xii) Falling Eye-Sight- This is also a common complaint in the last phase of pregnancy which also gets cured after the delivery. Some exercises, given ahead would help the lady to check her eyesight falling. Even otherwise, it must be understood that there are the travails that the lady has to undergo to acquire the exalted status of motherhood.

(xiii) Bleeding Gums - Owing to enhanced blood circulations, many ladies feel as if their gums have become rather fat and big which do bleed when they brush their teeth. In this stage it is advisable to use very soft brush or resort to the old practice of cleaning your teeth with tooth-powder or tooth-paste applied on your finger.

Since most of these changes are reversible type, the lady shouldn't get unduely worried about them. With patience and peace she can easily cope with these changes.

A Tabulated Chart to Confirm Pregnancy by Symptoms

I Normal Symptoms	*Time of Appearance*
1. Missed Period	3 to 10 days
2. Increased frequency of urination	2 to 3 weeks
3. Pain or tenderness in the breasts	2 to 3 weeks
4. Nausea and vomiting	2 to 3 weeks
5. Changes in the genital organs	2 to 3 weeks
6. Movement of the baby (quickening) felt	16 to 20 weeks
II Other Probable Symptoms	*Time of Appearance*
1. Rise in temperature	3 to 5 days
2. Chemical Changes (Characteristic of pregnancy)	1 to 2 weeks
3. Softening of the Cervix	4 to 6 weeks
4. Changes in the Uterus	4 plus weeks
5. Softening of the isthmus of the uterus	6 plus weeks
6. Enlargement of the abdomen	12 plus weeks
7. Feeling of the limb of the baby on palpation	20 plus weeks
8. Movement of the baby (displacement like a ball)	20 to 25 weeks

The Sure Symptoms Confirming Pregnancy

III Sure Symptoms	*Time of Appearance*
1. Audibility of the heart beats of the baby	20 to 24 weeks
2. Feeling of movements of the limbs of the baby by the mother	14 to 17 weeks
3. Appearance of the body of the baby in ultrasound	16 to 20 weeks

Antenatal Care

It is the dream of every couple that they should have healthy children. This dream can come true. It is all in your hands.

To ensure good health of your child, you should know that the care starts even before the child is born. In simple words, it means that every pregnant woman must take good care of herself. What you need to do is to follow certain simple rules. For your benefit, certain important points are emphasised here:

1. As soon as you think you are pregnant, get yourself registered at the earliest in an antenatal clinic(ANC) in the nearby hospital/dispensary/health centre/sub-centre.
2. Attend this clinic as advised by the health worker. You must go for atleast 3-check ups in this ANC. One at the time of registration, second in the 24-28 weeks and the third 3-4 weeks before the expected date of delivery.

During these visits, you will be examined thoroughly by the health worker, your height, weight and blood pressure will be taken and certain necessary investigations (e.g., haemoglobin estimation and urine examination) will also be carried out. If anything is found to be wrong, necessary management will be done by the health worker.

3. "High-Risk Mothers" need to visit the ANC more frequently as chances of problems arising in pregnancy are more.

You are a " High-Risk Mother" if you have even one of the following features :

- Age less than 18 years or more than 35 years.
- Height 140 cms or less.
- Bleeding through vagina or pain in abdomen during pregnancy (indicating threatened abortion).
- Anaemia (the tongue and nails look pale). Swelling of feet, high blood pressure and proteins in urine during pregnancy (indicating "pre-eclampsia") or convulsions during pregnancy besides all above symptoms (indicating "eclampsia")
- Twins
- History of Caesarean operation or forceps delivery.
- Malpresentations (i.e., the baby's position in the uterus is abnormal).
- Pregnancy associated with general diseases, e.g., heart disease, high blood pressure, kidney disease, diabetes, tuberculosis and liver disease, etc.
- If you are over 30 years of age and becoming pregnant for the first time.

4. You must take injections of Tetanus Toxoid (T.T.) during pregnancy. If it is your first pregnancy, take 2 injections of T.T. with a gap of 4-6 weeks between them. These injections can be taken anytime during pregnancy and are very essential to protect you and your new-born against a deadly disease called Tetanus.

If it is your second pregnancy and it has occurred within 3 years of the first pregnancy, you need to take only one injection of T.T. provided you had taken 2 injections of T.T. in the first pregnancy. If not, you need to take 2 injections.

5. Don't forget to take Folifer (Iron and Folic Acid) tablets. These tablets, taken one per day after meals, will prevent occurrence of anaemia in pregnancy. Anaemia means that haemoglobin—the red substance—in your

blood is low. Iron tablets can cause constipation in some people and can also make the stools black. Do not worry about the colour of stools. You may need to change the type of iron tablets if constipation persists. Consult the Health Worker.

If you already suffer from Anaemia, you will require two tablets every day taken 12 hours apart.

With this, take care of your diet as advised .

6. Take a nutritious and balanced diet.

Compared to your pre-pregnancy stage, you require atleast 50% more food during pregnancy. This is because of a rapidly growing baby inside your uterus. Remember if you eat well, the baby inside "eats" well and will be born with a good birth weight.

Increase your food intake by at least 50%. Do include lots of green, leafy vegetables (e.g., spinach, methi) for iron; fresh seasonal fruits for vitamins; jaggery for energy and gram (chana)/peas(matar) and pulses for proteins—the body building nutrients—in your diet. If possible, take atleast 2 glasses (total 500 ml) of milk and 1-2 eggs every day.

You should also remember that costly food items are not always more nutritious.

7. Have rest and sleep of 8 hours at night and if possible, and two hours in the afternoon.
8. Don't smoke or drink. Also make sure that others don't smoke in your vicinity. Smoking—whether active or passive—is extremely harmful for your un-born baby.
9. Don't take any medicines unless prescribed by a good, qualified doctor. Similarly, don't get investigations like X-ray and Ultrasound done on your own. All these can be harmful.
10. Keep yourself neat and clean. Take a daily bath. Be cheerful.
11. Keep your breasts clean. Wash them daily. Pregnancy is also the time to learn from the health worker about the technique for proper breast-feeding. If nipples of your breasts are inverted (facing inwards), this also

is the time to deal with this problem. Even before you consult a health worker for this problem, you can try to gently pull them out and hold them in this position for a few minutes. This procedure can be done 5-6 times every day.

12. If possible, sexual intercourse is better avoided in first 3 months and last 6 weeks of pregnancy.
13. Be vigilant. Report to the health worker/health facility, if you have any of these symptoms. These are danger signals and need immediate attention

A few weeks before the expected date of delivery, also plan about your delivery in advance. It is important that your delivery is conducted only by a trained health worker—in a clean and safe environment.

It is also important to find out about the nearest hospital where you can be taken in case there is a problem during delivery. Also, don't forget to arrange for a vehicle to be made available to you in case you are required to be shifted to a hospital.

Some Sure Sysmptoms of Trouble During Pregnancy

(i) Constant or recurring pain in the lower abdomen means some abnormality or malfunction in the uterus, which can result in miscarriage.

(ii) Before the expected end of term a discharge of clear fluid mixed with a little blood may be taken as a precursor of a miscarriage or premature delivery.

(iii) Painful and frequent urination (micturition) may be a sure sign of urinary or renal (Kidney) infections.

(iv) Swelling of the feet, or the joints of the fingers, knees etc. with puffiness of the face—a condition called' Oedema'—is also a bad sign. Reduction in the intake of salt and taking diuretics (the medication that induces frequent urination), if necessary, are generally sufficient to relieve the condition.

(v) If during the first eight weeks of pregnancy there is bleeding accompanied by recurring or continuous pain, as if caused by a sharp pointed object, there is a possibility that a miscarriage may occur. A pinkish discharge from the vagina in the twenty-eighth week indicates some abnormality or malfunction in the uterus.

(vi) A rise in the temperature of the body of a pregnant woman should always be treated with utmost concern. Any fever in this stage may disturb the process and may create unnecessary complication. The pregnant woman should be always aware of this fact.

(vii) Frequent vomiting accompanied by no or very little water or liquids must warrant an immediate medical attention. If the woman is unable to retain food in the stomach, it sends danger signal to its retaining the foetus also.

During 24 hours preceding the delivery, generally, no movements of the baby are felt, because it is in a state. In case no movement are felt for more than 48 hours, consulting a doctor is a must, that too immediately.

General Care of the Body

During pregnancy, as explained earlier, the abdomen becomes larger, and the skin stretches, fibres of connective tissues immediately underlying the skin separate and give rise to white stretch marks. To avoid this, it is always wise to massage the abdomen and breasts regularly with oil (specially the oil containing Vitamin E) from the first month of pregnancy right to the last and even after delivery—for a few months at least. On no account scratch the abdomen and the breasts, because this will leave scratch marks forever afterwards on the skin. If you feel itchy, rub the skin gently with your hands.

In case you are planning on breast feeding your baby, start preparing your nipples from the sixth month onwards. Once everyday, draw out nipples by gently pressing your thumb and index finger down on either side of the nipple and gently rolling the nipple out. After your nipples stand out, massage it with little olive oil. Nursing will not cause your breasts to become flabby, if you wear well-fitting brassieres. Buy yourself a few maternity dresses which today come in many attractive designs and shapes. Don't forget that a large percentage of attractiveness is accounted for by good grooming and good posture.

The clothes should be comfortable and well fitting with allowance for future expansion. Also discard high-heeled shoes and wear comfortable low-heeled flat shoes/sandles.

Towards the later months many pregnant women

develop varicose veins in which the veins become very much enlarged and protrude out of skin. These veins develop in such conditions mostly in legs. The women who develop this condition are the ones whose job requirement is to keep standing for long hours.

It is always advisable during pregnancy that the lady should do as much of her work as possible in a sitting position with her feet properly popped up. When they have to be on their feet it is better to move around than to stand still. If you develop this condition, wear plastic stockings before you get up from your bed. Report you condition quickly to your doctor. Besides, you should lie down at least once every day for at least one hour in a body-slant position.

Sometimes swelling of legs, ankles, feet, fingers, face, toe, may appear during the last months. The cause of swelling is the retention of water in the tissue spaces of the body: a high intake of the salt favours the retention of water, so the intake of the salt should be reduced to the minimum. The liquid intake should also be reduced to as little as possible. But this might create constipation problem. Hence you should find the optimum intake of liquids and salts by your own experience. However, the pressure of the body on the large blood vessels in the later month may give rise occasionally to bouts of light-heartedness and fainting. If this occurs, you will feel better if you lie down for a few minutes. Also increase your intake of iron.

Many a time the sleep may be interrupted by hard muscular cramps in the calves of your legs. Massage the cramped areas vigorously and apply hot water bottle or heating pad to the area.

Another common complaints are heart burn and flatulence during the period of pregnancy. Heartburn is a kind of burning sensation which is noted at the lower end of the breast bone. Hence the name heartburn, to prevent this eat lighter meals at regular intervals rather than bigger meals after long intervals. Flatulence is the formation of gas in the body in large quantity. To avoid this have more nourishing than rich food.

Proper care of the skin and hair is specially important during pregnancy. A daily bath with a mild fragrant soap is a must. Clean your skin both morning and night with milk cream to which a little of lime juice and turmeric powder has been added. Every morning before you go in for your bath, take a spoonful of curd and mix a few drops each of almond oil and the essence of rose. Rub well into the skin and remove with cotton-wool. This will soothe and feed the skin.

In the night rub your skin with a skin solution prepared in the following way : add one teaspoonful each of almond oil, cucumber juice, honey, rose water and lime juice. Mix well and put in a small jar and store either in the fridge or a cool, dry place. Apply it every night before going to bed. Remove in the morning with a piece of cotton-wool, then splash on cold water. This will remove the bloom on your cheeks and make your complexion sparkling.

Some ladies, to hide the blemishes on the face, wear very heavy make up. This is wrong. They should wear a minimum possible make up. In case the lady has a tendency to develop rashes, it would be accentuated during this period. Sometimes pigmentation of the skin takes place or a formation in small area in which the minute skin veins become prominent. There is nothing to worry about them as they would automatically disappear after the delivery.

The Causes of Repeated Abortions and Miscarriage

(i) Lifting a very heavy object.
(ii) Running or jumping in great speed.
(iii) All of a sudden the two feet of the woman falling on different levels; climbing high or mounting high steps.
(iv) Having very hot drinks or eating very hot foods.
(v) Having the muscles of the ovaries rather loose causing its mouth to open soon, at little exertion.

(vi) Having the husband's sperm or your ovum's inherent strength very weak.
(vii) Being anaemic or having some blood deficiency or having an inherent incompatibility between the husband's or your's blood groups.
(ix) Being too chicken hearted and timid by nature to withstand any trauma or shock or sudden explosion of sound.

Besides these your husband's, callousness to care for your comfort and safety or his being reckless during coitus while you are pregnant are the other potential causes of your aborting or miscarry.

A lady has to be extremely careful about these pitfalls and should take every precaution to avoid them.

Abnormal Foetus Position

There are certain abnormal cases, in which the buttocks of a baby are in the pelvis or the baby may be lying across the uterus.

In such cases, the doctors advise a Caesarean section, but, in homoeopathy, there is a medicine which puts the foetus into its normal head down position in the uterus. In a majority of cases, this medicine has proved successful.

The treatment takes a minimum of fifteen days to effects the change. And, if that much time is available, one must go in for homoeopathic treatment to avoid caesarean delivery. I have treated a number of such cases and the success rate was more than 90%.

"PULSATILLA" IN 1M(1000) potency is the medicine for such cases, to be taken one dose every morning on an empty stomach for a period of three days. Try and see the magic.

However, in cases, where the passage is small and the passenger is big, there is no alternative to a caesarean operation.

The first three months of pregnancy are crucial because, as mentioned earlier, it is during this period that the baby's organs—brain, heart, kidneys, eyes, ears and other limbs are formed. No medicine should be taken during this period unless there are some developments, threatening at abortion or the mother's life.

Exercise During Pregnancy

It is a mistaken belief that pregnancy is an ordeal through which the woman emerges only after losing her physical beauty, her charms, her contours and her curve. A well balanced diet with regular exercise can make her preserve her charms and the post-pregnancy exercise and dietary regimes can turn her into a new woman.

During pregnancy many changes in the body occur.

The body becomes heavy and fat, the stomach or lower abdomen gets rather protruded. All these changes disturb the lady's equilibrium because some of her muscles had to work under stress. Owing to various reasons of comfort and convenience, most of the pregnant ladies develop wrong gait and stance which put further load on their muscles. First of all they must learn how to walk or carry themselves without putting least burden upon their body.

How to Stand and Sit

Right equilibrium of the body means carrying it without putting any extra burden on your muscles and bones. Owing to the extra pressure on the spine due to heavier portion of the stomach, an unwanted arch at the back is developed which overstretches the tendons and muscles at the back and the sides. As the baby develops in the womb, the abdomen of the expectant mother progressively bulges forward. This bulge creates tension in the muscles of the back and waist. It is this sign that is responsible for the usual upright appearance which also causes the backache. In order to lessen the tension she should repeatedly try to constrict her hip muscles towards inside. Moreover, she must also learn the right way of standing or sitting. Given below are the pictorial illustrations of doing so rightly.

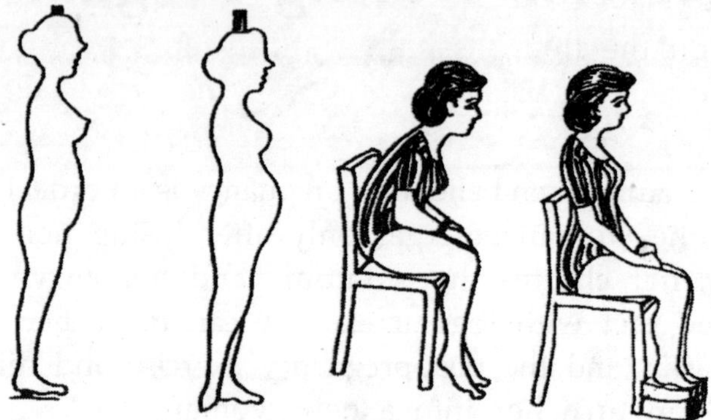

Right way   Wrong way   Right way   Wrong way

How to Sit and Stand (For Pregnant Ladies & for non pregnant too)

Since most of the time the pregnant lady keeps sitting, she must know how to sit properly. Never allow your legs to hang in the air. They ought to be given a support by providing adequately high footrest if, while sitting on the chair her legs are left hanging

Now do the following exercise to improve your stance

(a) Lie flat on the floor and bend the legs from the knees so that your feet remain firmly on the floor. Now constricting your back and abdomen muscles gradually try to make your back fully touch the floor. Count 5 to 10 and then relax your body.

Now raising your head and shoulders a bit, constrict again your stomach muscles and try to touch your left toe with your right hand. Then reverse the exercise and try to touch your right toe with the left hand. Repeat it for about 5 to 10 times.

Now sit on the floor with both the legs stretched and turn your feet from ankles as much upwards as possible. Repeat it for 8 to 10 times. Now rotate your feet in a circular motion. Do it for 8 to 10 times. This exercise reduces swelling on the feet and the cramps in the muscles.

(b) *Exercises for Strengthening the Abdomen*

With knees slightly apart, kneel down and place your palms on the floor, assuming an all-fours position. Now maintaining your balance and keeping the back straight. raise the right arm and the left leg till they are level with your back. Return to the initial position, perform the same movement with the left arm and the right leg. Repeat ten times for each side alternately.

(c) *Exercise for Strengthening the Back Muscles*

With face up, lie on the floor. Then gradually bending the legs at the knee, try to bring the feet nearer the torso. Press down with one foot so as to raise the back off the floor. Maintain this position for six seconds. Return to the the initial position. Now do the same with the other foot. Now press down with both feet simultaneously to raise the back off the floor. Maintain this position for six seconds. Return to the initial position. Repeat the whole sequence ten times. In case you feel it putting strain on you, relax a bit and then perform this exercise.

(d) *Exercise to Provide Relief in the Backache*

Lie down flat with face up on the floor. Bend the legs at the knees. Now raise the back off the floor, with arms extended forward and reach for the knees. Keeping the back thus raised, impart a rotatory motion to the hips. Keep this up for six seconds, without lowering the back. Now bring yourself down very gently to the initial position. Giving pauses repeat the entire sequence of movement ten times.

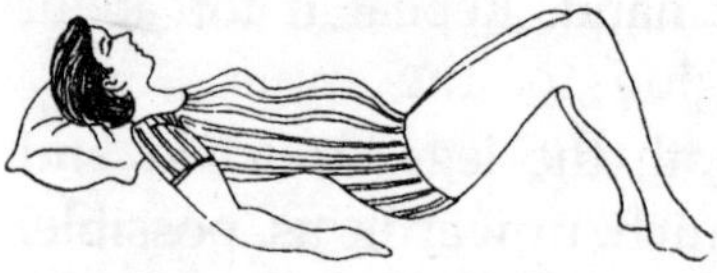

Exercise to prevent Backache

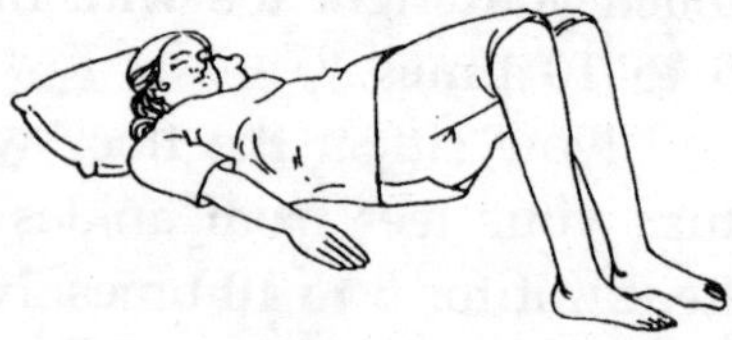

Excercise to prevent swelling of feet

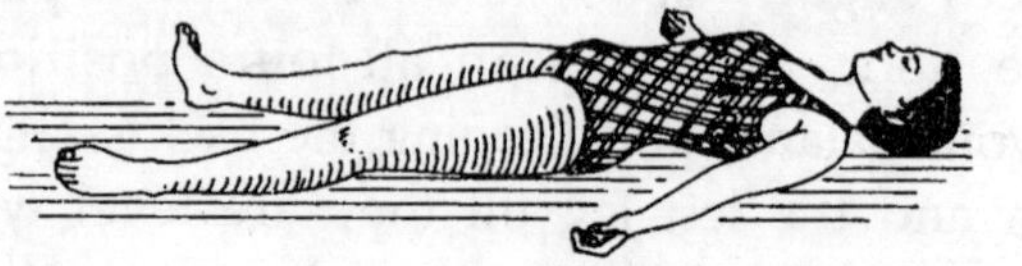

Shavasana

Exercises for the Pregnant Woman

(e) *Another Exercise for Relieving Backache*

Kneel down on the floor, and bend forward, assuming an all four-position. Supporting yourself on the palms placed directly beneath the shoulders, and on the toes of the feet, raise the knees off the floor, Raise the back, keeping the head down. Do not let the back sag down. Maintain this position for six seconds. Return to the all fours position. Repeat the sequence of movements five to six times without unduly exerting your body.

There is also another way of doing this exercise. Sit on a flat chair with a straight upright back. Place the palms on the knees. Now push the elbow outwards, without shifting the palms. This will put the abdominal muscles under tension. Maintain the tension for six seconds, then relax slowly repeat it ten times.

Note—It is not necessary to do all of these exercises. The pregnant lady should choose the exercise she is able to perform without any trouble. The point is not doing a lot of exercises, do a few selected ones but regularly.

(f) *Exercises for Controlling Excessive Bulging of the Abdomen as also for reliving Backache*

Backache is the most common complaint of the pregnant women, specially in the lower regions of the spine. Some of them develop this complaint after delivery. The exercises given below would prove greatly beneficial in such cases. Initially perform these exercise for five times a day and then their frequency could be raised to 20 a day—again if you don't feel strain.

(i) Frame yourself inside a doorway about 2.5 to 3 feet wide with the buttocks against one side of the door frame. Keep the ankles 4 inches apart. Press against the frame with the back. Tense up the muscles of the buttocks and the abdomen which will have the effect of bending legs a little at the knees, and of inclining the pelvis forwards.

Having done so press against the door frame behind you with the nape, and push against the frame of the door facing you with the palms. Now straighten the legs at the knees. Then relax your body muscles and take a break . In case you feel thirsty, wait for some time to normalise your breath and then have some lukewarm drink. Having fortified yourself, do it few more times without straining yourself unduly.

(ii) Lie flat on the floor with your face up. Let the soles of the feet rest flat on the floor with legs comfortably bent at the knees. Raise your legs, grasp the knees and pull it as near to the chest as you possibly can. Hold on to this position for 5 seconds. Then regain the initial position. Repeat it with the other leg and alternately do this exercise for about 10 times. In doing all these exercises, make sure that there is no pressure building up on your abdomen. This is important.

(iii) Again lie flat on the floor with your face up. As in the earlier exercise bend your legs from the knees to let your sole rest flat on the floor, bend the arms at the elbows and place them under the head. Now tighten the muscles of the waist and the abdomen in such a way that the lower part of the back presses firmly on the floor. Hold your body in this position for five seconds or so and then relax the muscles of your entire body Repeat for 4 to 5 times the whole sequence of the exercise.

(iv) Lie on the floor in the same way as you did in the earlier exercise. Bend the knees and let the soles of the feet rest flat on the floor. Raise the legs, grasp both the knees with your hands and pull them as near to the chest as you can. Hold the position for five seconds and resume the initial position. Straighten the legs and repeat the movement for about 4 to 5 times.

Note—As is the medical fact, between the bones in the joints, and the tendons attaching the muscles to the bones tend to soften after the delivery. Strengthening the muscles will help maintain the elasticity and strength of these tissues, and minimise the softening. Most of the above described exercises have been devised to strengthen the muscles that are involved thus reducing the possibility of the consequent pain.

The expectant mother must perform these exercises just as soon as she learns that she is pregnant she would of course be well advised to observe moderation in the matter, taking care that the quantum or the pace of the exercise should not cause fatigue of any kind. The benefits of these exercises become apparent in the later stages of pregnancy when the abdomen begins to sag forward.

(g) *Breathing Exercises-Breathing exercises are also very essential during the period of pregnancy*

(i) Sit comfortably on the normal squanting pose i.e. with your knees bent and one foot kept over one thigh and the other under it. Now keep your hands softly on your stomach and leave a deep sigh while distending your stomach as much as possible . Now exhale . Repeat the process at least 5 to 6 times a day.

(ii) Normally during the period of pregnancy the lady is prone to getting tired very soon. Hence give sufficient pauses between each exercise and do yogsanas like Shavasana.

Shavasana- This classic, simple yet difficult, exercise is to be performed in the end of every exercise session. Since it ensures complete relaxation of the body and spirit, after it no other exercise should be performed. This asana is called shavasana or the Corpse Posture because it initiate the dead body or corpse and provides relaxation to the muscles and the mind. The technique of it is as follows :

Lie flat on your back, keeping your body totally relaxed. Keep the hands at a little distance from the thighs, with palm upwards. Let the feet lie at about one to one and a half a feet. Keep your eyes closed. Now take a deep breath and then breath slowly, evenly and rhythmically so as not to disturb your body's posture. Inhalations should be equal and uniform. There should be no effort to increase the volume of respiration. A rhythmic breathing is all that is required. Now concentrate on your respiration and relax completely. Keep the jaws loose and not detached. Let there be no movement either of the pupils of the eye or of the tongue.

In the beginning you may fall asleep but when by practice you immerse into deep relaxation you would feel your body and mind in peace, and completely relaxed. In shavasana, the main effort is of the concentration of the mind. Select mentally any part of your body, preferably starting from your feet, and by autosuggestion start feeling as though your feet has become senseless or dead. Then come to shins, to knees to thighs etc. up your head. By the time you reach up to your head in your mental concentration you would be in a sort of rejuvenating stupor. Repeat constantly in your mind : I relax my feet and they are relaxed, I relax my legs and they are relaxed etc, concentrating on each of your external body part one by one. The head (brain) may come up the last. This way one by one you relax your entire body.

BENEFITS—Shavasana removes all fatigue caused by other asanas and induces a tranquillity, feeling a calmness of mind. It makes one feel one's mind to be akin to a deep and still pool of clean water, . Mentally dive deep into this pool and emerge refreshed and relaxed.

Steady, smooth, even, uniform and undisturbed respiration soothes nerves, muscles and calms brain. It reduces high blood pressure, a common complaint during pregnancy, and tension and fatigue. The whole nervous system gets toned up.

Fetal Development and Emotions

The terms used to date a pregnancy can be confusing. Once the pregnancy is confirmed, your caregiver will estimate your due date by counting from the first day of your last menstrual period. Since fertilization took place approximately 2 weeks after your period, you are considered as having been 2 weeks pregnant at the time of fertilization. Throughout your pregnancy, your progress will be measured in weeks of gestation (pregnancy) and the baby will be given a gestational age as measured from the first day of your last menstrual period. For example, when you are 12 weeks pregnant, the fetus is actually only 10 weeks old but is referred to as a 12-week-old fetus or as begin at 12 weeks gestational age.

Pregnancy is also divided into three trimesters, each consisting of 3 calendar months. In addition, lunar months are used to describe events occurring during the pregnancy. A lunar month equals 28 days, and a pregnancy lasts 10 lunar months.

Most of the development of the fetal organs takes place during the first trimester. At the beginning of this phase, the ovum is a single cell. By the end of the twelth week or third lunar month, the fetus is recognizable as a human and the placenta is fully functioning exchanging nutrients and waste products. The second trimester is a time of continued development. Most of the fetal growth and maturation of the organs takes place during the third trimester.

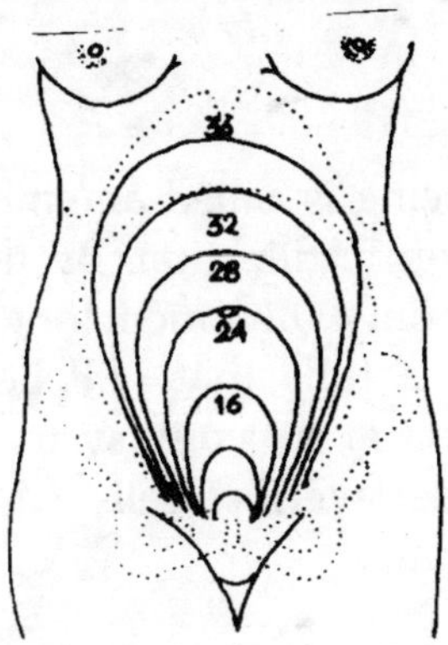

Increase in size of foetus from 16-36 weeks as seen from outside on abdomen

First Week

During the first week following fertilization, the single cell or ovum, as the developing being is called for the first weeks, divides again and again, forming a hollowing ball three cell layers. Projections, called villi, appear on the outside of the ovum and help the ovum to burrow into the uterus usually on the upper back wall.

Second Week

By the end of the second week following fertilization, the hollow space in the ovum has acquired two parts — an amniotic sac, which is filled with fluid, and a yolk sac, which will produce small blood vessels and cells. The yolk sac will degenerate as the developing being begins producing its own blood cells. The amniotic sac has three functions — protecting the developing being from shocks, keeping the temperature constant, and serving as a barrier against infection from the outside. It is composed of two membranes that will eventually fuse together. The amnion, or inner layer, produces the amniotic fluid and the chlorin forms the outer layer.

Third Week

The developing being is called an embryo from the third to the eighth week after fertilization. By the end of the third week, the embryo is only 0.11 inch long. It has buds that will grow into lungs, a tube that will become a heart and the beginning of a central nervous system. All of these are growing from the three layers of cells. Most pregnancy tests are positive at this time.

Fourth Week

By the end of the fourth week after fertilization or 6 week gestational age, the embryo is 0.19 inch long. The nervous system and brain are beginning to grow, and the face is forming, with a mouth, a lower jaw, and dark circles where the eyes will be. The heart is beating and is pumping blood around the developing blood vessels. Little buds that will become the arms and legs have appeared.

Fifth Week

By the end of the fifth week after fertilization or 7 weeks gestational age, the embryo is 0.5 inch long. The brain, spinal cord, and nervous system are more developed. The head had increased in size, and the nostrils, lips, and tongue are visible. The limb buds have grown into arms and legs.

Sixth Week

By the end of the sixth week after fertilization or 8 weeks gestational age, the embryo is 0.9 inch long. The head is quite large in comparison to the trunk. External ears form elevations on either side of the head. A skeleton made of cartilage, not real bone, has appeared; and a tail is apparent at the end of the spinal cord. Fingers and toes have formed.

Seventh Week

The embryo is almost an inch in length by the end of the seventh week after fertilization or 9 weeks gestational age. The brain can be seen through the fine skin on the top of the head. The eyes are visible through the closed lids. The body may begin to move as small muscle fibres grow. Bone has begun to replace the cartilage and the tail has almost disappeared. The embryo is now uniquely human, with most of the internal organs present.

Eighth Week

From the eighth week after fertilization or 10 weeks gestational age, until birth, the developing baby is called a fetus. By the end of the eighth week, the fetus is approximately $1\frac{1}{2}$ inches long and weighs about 2 grams. The jaws and other facial features are more clearly developed, and teeth are forming. The arms begin to bend at the elbow and are long enough for the baby to touch his face. If the baby is a boy, his penis is apparent. If the baby is a girl, her clitoris has developed.

Ninth Week

By the end of the ninth week after fertilization or 11 weeks gestational age, the fetus looks more human. It measures almost 2 inches in length and weighs 4 grams (1/6 ounce). Most of the major structures have formed. Development now consists of the growth and maturing of present structures. The scrotum has appeared, as have fingernails, toe-nails and hair follicles.

Third Lunar Month

By the end of the third lunar month or 12 weeks gestational age, the fetus is over $2\frac{1}{2}$ inches in length and weighs 7 grams (1/3 ounce). The face is well developed, with the eyelids present, though fused. The baby can move the muscles of his face to squint, purse his lips and open his mouth. The arms, hands, fingers, legs, feet, and toes are fully developed. The external genitalia show definite signs of male or female sex. The baby can make a fist and kick with his feet, although the woman cannot feel it yet. The uterus can be felt just above the woman's pubic bone. The fetal heartbeat can be heard with a doptone, the device used by caregivers to listen to babies.

Fourth Lunar Month

By the end of the fourth lunar month or 16 weeks gestational age, the fetus is, almost 5 inches long and weighs 100 grams (3 ounces). The essential body systems are now present; most of the remaining changes will be in size. To facilitate this growth, the placenta is also growing rapidly. The baby's skin is getting thicker and less transparent and is forming several layers. Eyebrows and eyelashes are evident. The baby may suck his thumb and he may swallow amniotic fluid and then pass it out as urine. Meconium, the baby's first bowel movement, is beginning to collect in his intestinal tract. Some women feel the first faint fluttering movements between their pubic bone and navel. These movements are often initially confused with gas, but the feeling is "quickening," the earliest felt movements of a fetus. Usually, quickening is first perceived between the sixteenth and eighteenth weeks.

Fifth Lunar Month

By the end of the fifth lunar month or 20 weeks gestational age, the fetus is about 8 inches long and weighs

240 grams. Some fat has been deposited under his skin, but he is still quite thin. His skin is less transparent. Hair has appeared on his head, and downy hair called lanugo is covering his body. This is the midpoint of pregnancy.

Sixth Lunar Month

By the end of the sixth lunar month or 24 weeks gestational age, the fetus is almost 11 inches long and weighs 500 grams (1 pound 2 ounces). Vernix caseosa, a cheeselike coating that protects the baby's skin from its watery environment, has developed. The eyes are open, and the fetus can hear. Fingerprints and footprints have formed. Between 40 and 60 percent of the babies born at this time survive.

Seventh Lunar Month

By the end of the seventh lunar month or 28 weeks gestational age, the baby is close to 13 inches long and weighs about 900 grams (2 pounds). The eyes can perceive light and the baby can hear, smell, taste, and respond to touch. The baby has definite awake and sleep periods. If the baby is a boy, his testicles have descended into his scrotum. Over 90 percent of the babies born at this point survive.

Eighth Lunar Month

By the end of the eighth lunar month or 32 weeks gestational age, the average baby, is 15 inches long and weighs 1,500 grams (3 pounds 5 ounces) or more. The skin is still red but is less wrinkled and the fingernails are long. If born now, the baby's chance of survival is better than 95 percent.

Ninth Lunar Month

By the end of the ninth lunar month or 36 weeks gestational age, the baby is almost 17 inches long and weighs between

2,160 grams (4 pounds 12 ounces) and 2,500 grams (5 pounds 9 ounces). During the last 2 months of gestation, the baby gains about an ounce of weight a day. This weight gain is important because it provides the baby with a layer of fat under his skin that will help keep his body temperature constant outside the uterus. The skin has become smoother, and the redness has faded to pink. Most of the lanugo has dropped off, remaining only on the arms and shoulders. The lungs are maturing and are producing lecithin, which is necessary for respiration.

Tenth Lunar Month

By the end of the tenth lunar month or 40 weeks gestational age, the baby's brain has greatly increased in number of cells. This growth will continue for the first 5 to 6 months after birth. By now, 96 percent of all babies are positioned head down. During the final 2 to 4 weeks of gestation, the head or other presenting part settles down into the top of the woman's pelvis. During this last lunar month, the baby gains about 1/2 pound per week and, by the fortieth week, is an average of 20 inches in length and 7 to 7 1/2 pounds in weight. The baby is ready to be bom!

FETAL EMOTIONS

We now know that even while all of this physical development is taking place, the unborn child is becoming an aware, reacting human being. At as early as 8 weeks, he can express his likes and dislikes with well-placed kicks and jerks. At 28 to 32 weeks, his emerging sense of awareness transforms his physical responses into feelings. The woman's emotional state can and does have an effect on the way he perceives his world—as warm and friendly, or cold and hostile. This is not to say that fleeting anxiety or doubt about your health will negatively affect your unborn child. However, it does mean the chronic anxiety or stress, especially of a personal nature, or deep ambivalence about motherhood may affect your baby's personality.

Studies have shown that the unborn child hears well from the twenty-fourth week on. A recent discovery is that the noise level inside the uterus is much higher than was previously thought. The woman's constant heartbeat and intestinal rumblings are magnified by the amniotic fluid, providing a continuous, loud, and rhythmical background for the baby. The kinds of sounds a baby hears definitely affect him emotionally. Soft, soothing sounds and music calm him; loud sounds and music such as hard rock can make him kick violently. Some women have found that if they play soft music when resting during the last months of pregnancy, the baby, after he is born, associates this music with rest time.

The exciting aspect of this knowledge about fetal emotions is that you can begin shaping a positive relationship with your child before he is born. Talk soothingly to your baby and send him loving thoughts. This is also a good way to get your partner involved in the pregnancy. Encourage your partner to gently massage your abdomen and to talk to his baby as well. Try to spend a portion of each day in a relaxed, anxiety-free state of mind. Both you and your unbom child will benefit.

The Placenta

By the time the developing being is 2 weeks old, the placenta has begun to develop. The villi, embedded in the lining of the uterus, are forming primitive blood vessels, which tap into the woman's blood supply. The function of the placenta is to supply the growing being with the oxygen and nutrients it needs from the woman's blood system and to pass to the woman the waste products it does not need.

The fetal blood is always separate from the maternal blood. Substances are passed back and forth through a semipermeable membrane. At one time, the placenta was thought to act as a barrier to materials that might hurt the fetus. However, it is now known that almost everything that enters the woman's body—including viruses, drugs, nicotine and alcohol—is passed to the fetus.

The placenta continues to grow until about 2 months before delivery, when it reaches its maximum size. At that time, it is about the size and shape of a dinner plate, approximately 8 to 9 inches in diameter, but thicker and heavier, weighing I to 2 pounds at birth. The side that is attached to the uterine wall is dark red and has sections like circular puzzle pieces in it. Scar like areas of tissue may be apparent. These are areas of calcification and they denote places that have degenerated. Women who smoke during pregnancy have more of these than do women who do not smoke. The side of the placenta that is next to the fetus is white and smooth, being covered by a membrane, the amniotic sac.

Nutrients coming from the woman pass to the blood vessels in the placenta. From the placenta, they move through the umbilical cord into the blood circulating within the fetus.

Inside the umbilical cord are three blood vessels—one large vein and two smaller arteries. Nutrients travel from the placenta to the fetus through the vein. Waste products return to the placenta through the arteries to be passed into the woman's system. A jelly like substance called Wharton's jelly surrounds the blood vessels and helps to protect them.

The umbilical cord begins to develop during the second week after conception and usually grows to about 18 inches in length, although it is possible for it to grow to anywhere from 12 inches to 40 inches. After the birth of the baby, the cord is clamped and cut. A stump remains, but dries up and falls off in 7 to 10 days.

LENGTH OF PREGNANCY

The average length of pregnancy is 280 days. This is about 9 calendar months or 10 lunar months. A lunar month is the time it takes to go from full in full moon-28 days.

Your doctor calculated your estimated due date by adding 7 days to the first day of your last normal menstrual period and then counting back 3 months. For example, if the first day of your last menstrual period was February 15, he added 7 days, which brought the date to February 22, the subtracted 3 months, for an expected due date of November 22. This is about 280 days after February 15. The baby would be only about 266 days old on November 22, but the date of the last menstrual period is used because the actual date of conception is usually unknown and could be as early as day or 6 of the menstrual cycle. Only about 4 percent of women carry their babies for exactly 280 days, but 66 percent deliver within 10 days before or after their due dates. The due date is only an estimate, based on an average of all pregnancies. Your baby may take more or less time to develop, the sarne way that some babies take more or less time to get their first tooth.

Physical and Emotional Changes in the Woman

Pregnancy is generally divided into three trimesters or three periods of 3 months each, for purposes of discussion. This is done because most women experience the same general changes during each trimester.

During pregnancy, two kinds of development go on at once—the physical changes in the mother-to-be and the physical changes in the fetus. Along with the physical changes the woman experiences, some emotional changes take place. You and your partner can use these changes as opportunities to grow, to expand your awareness of yourselves and of each other, to deepen your sense of responsibility and to become aware of what millions of other parents have experienced.

FIRST TRIMESTER

The first trimester of pregnancy is the first 3 calendar months or through the fourteenth week of gestation. You will experience many physical and emotional changes during this time, although most of the physical changes will be more noticeable to you than to anyone else.

Physical Changes

The major physical changes that women experience during the first trimester include the following:

Uterus **:** For many women, a missed menstrual period is the first sign of pregnancy. Other women continue to have very light periods for the first 2 to 3 months. This lack of a regular period is due to the high levels of estrogen and progesterone that the body produces to maintain the uterine lining that nourishes the developing embryo. Many women spot slightly on the day the ovum attaches itself to the uterine wall. This is not menstrual bleeding; rather, it is called implantation bleeding.

By the time the fetus is 12 weeks old, the placenta or afterbirth, has formed. The uterus has grown to the size of a grapefruit, with its top reaching to just above the pubic bone. The cervix has already begun softening.

Vagina **:** The vagina has begun thickening and softening because of the increase in maternal hormones. It has also turned blue to violet in colour as a result of the increased blood supply to the area. Vaginal secretions have become more noticeable and will increase in amount as the pregnancy progresses.

Breasts **:** A tingling or prickling sensation is often felt in the breasts during the early weeks of pregnancy. This is because the blood supply is increasing and the milk-secreting glands are growing. After a few weeks or months, the tingling or prickling will disappear, but the breasts will usually continue to enlarge until the third trimester.

Around the eighth week, veins may become visible under the skin, and small round elevated areas appear on the aureola, the dark area surrounding the nipple. These elevated areas are the Montgomery glands, which secrete oil to help keep the nipples soft and pliable in preparation for breastfeeding.

Urination **:** Many women experience an increased need to urinate during the first trimester because the enlarging uterus is pressing on the bladder. This need usually eases during the second trimester, as the uterus rises out of the pelvis. Even though it means more trips to the bathroom, you should drink plenty of fluids to maintain good kidney function and to provide the water necessary to metabolize the protein you eat.

Digestion : About half of all pregnant women feel nauseated and may vomit during early pregnancy and sometimes also in later pregnancy. This condition is called morning sickness, although it can occur at any time during the day. Morning sickness is attributed to an increase in hormone levels, a lack of vitamin B6, and or low blood sugar. Eating foods high in the B vitamins and consuming small high-protein meals throughout the day usually help this condition.

In addition to nausea, some women also have trouble with indigestion and heartburn. The hormones relaxin and progesterone relax the smooth muscles in the body, including the sphincter at the top of the stomach, which keeps food in the stomach. Progesterone is also responsible for relaxing the intestines somewhat, thereby slowing digestion and making constipation more likely. Eating a diet high in fiber (fresh fruits and vegetables and whole grains), drinking plenty of fluids, and exercising regularly help to minimize constipation.

Skin : The hormones of pregnancy can affect your skin either positively or negatively. Many women experience the glow of pregnancy and their skin radiates. Others are not so fortunate and develop acne. Continue to eat a good diet and drink plenty of water. Wash your face two or three times a day with a gentle cleanser and apply moisturizer to dry areas. Avoid the temptation to pick at or squeeze the blemishes. This will only increase the likelihood of infection and scarring. Choose makeup that does not clog the pores or try to limit the time you wear it. Wash the applicators or purchase new blush brush or powder "puffs." If the acne is severe, you may need to see a dermotologist. Make sure that he knows you are pregnant. Two common medications used for acne, Accutane and Retin A, should not be used during pregnancy (Allopathic medicines).

Fatigue : Pregnancy brings changes to every system in

the body and the changes require a great deal of physical and emotional energy. Proper rest is extremely important for an expectant mother. You should not feel guilty about resting during the day or about going to bed early. You need rest for your body to adjust to pregnancy.

Emotional Changes

Many expectant mothers spend the first trimester accepting the fact that they are pregnant and coming to terms with the implications. This is true for other family members as well. You may find yourself drawing inward and focusing on the changes in your body and on your fears and dreams. You may feel increasingly vulnerable to danger and may also fear miscarriage.

Even when the pregnancy is wanted, expectant parents usually have many questions: Can we afford a child'? How will our lifestyle change ? Will we have jealousy problems with our other children? The woman may wonder ? Will I quit work? Both parents-to-be may feel a sense of panic at the additional responsibilities. Ambivalent feelings toward the pregnancy are very common in the early months. These feelings are not bad or wrong. By acknowledging and talking about them, you and your partner may find yourselves better able to cope with them and to accept the pregnancy. Facing your doubts and fears about pregnancy aids in emotional growth.

Many couples enjoy more sexual activity during this time of adjustment while other couples may desire less sex. You and your partner should talk to each other openly about your feelings to prevent pent-up fears from damaging your relationship.

By the end of this first trimester, you may find that you have begun to sort out and examine your feelings toward your own parents. Think about how you will be different from or similar to them. Among the other feelings you may experience during the first trimester are excitement, increased creativity and increased sensuality. You may feel "special" during this time.

Mood swings sometimes become more extreme during pregnancy. You may find yourself laughing or crying over insignificant things. This problem is related to the increasing levels of hormones. Researchers believe that these hormones do not cause the moods, but probably increase the intensity of feelings. Some evidence has shown that expectant mothers feel more anxiety if the baby is a boy, but the reason for this is unknown.

Women experiencing a second or later pregnancy often find that they are less preoccupied with the pregnancy than they were with their first. The major adjustment to parenthood seems to come with a first pregnancy. With later pregnancies, women have less time available and feel less of a need to ponder the meaning of each physical change.

SECOND TRIMESTER

The second trimester of pregnancy is the middle 3 months or from the fifteenth through the twenty-eighth week of gestation. This trimester is often the most enjoyable of the three. Your initial period of adjustment has passed, and fatigue and nausea are usually less of a problem. It is during this time that your pregnancy becomes obvious to other people, and you may frequently be the centre of attention. Your body, though larger, is not cumbersome and you should find it fairly easy to move around.

Physical Changes

The major physical changes that women experience during the second trimester include the following:

Uterus :The uterus begins to expand out of the pelvis and into the abdominal cavity by the fourteenth week. By the twentieth week, which is midway through the second trimester, the uterus is usually at the level of the navel.

A woman pregnant for the first time usually begins to

feel the movements of the fetus at about 16 to 18 weeks. Women who have already borne at least one child often feel these movements earlier. When the movements are first perceived, the fetus is about 7 inches long and weighs less than I pound. The woman may also feel mild uterine contractions, called Braxton-Hicks contractions.

Vagina : The tissues of the vagina continue to soften and become more elastic, preparing for the baby's passage at birth.

Pelvis : Hormones cause the cartilage to soften and widen to provide additional mobility and relaxation in the pelvic joints. This allows a large baby to pass through more easily.

Breasts : Colostrum, a clear yellow fluid that precedes mature breastmilk, is often present by 16 weeks.

Circulation : By the end of the second trimester, the blood volume has increased by 40 to 60 percent and the heart has begun pumping more blood per beat. Edema (swelling) is common because of the increased blood volume, the pressure from the enlarging uterus, and the increase in estrogen. The fluid will tend to pool in your feet and hands when you stand for long periods. Resting on your side will improve your circulation and will help to relieve the edema. Increasing your protein intake will also help to decrease the swelling. If the swelling is sudden and involves the face, you should notify your doctor, since this may be a sign of pregnancy-induced hypertension.

Linea nigra : The linea nigra is a dark line that extends from the navel to the pubic hairline. It is common and is attributed to the hormonal activity of pregnancy. It fades after delivery, although it may continue to be visible.

Stretch marks : Many women develop at least some stretch marks, or striae gravidarum, during pregnancy. Stretch marks appear when the connective tissue of the skin is stretched to the point of rupture. They are red or pink lines and may appear on the abdomen, thighs, or breasts. After delivery, they fade to white. Many women find that massaging oil or lotion into the vulnerable areas prevents stretch marks, although heredity seems to be a more important factor.

Mask of pregnancy : Some women develop the mask of pregnancy, which consists of dark blotches on the face. This pigmentation is believed to result from increased levels of melanocyte stimulating hormone (MSH). Production of MSH drops after pregnancy, with the mask of pregnancy usually disappearing. Deficiency of folic acid, a B vitamin, may also be a cause. Your prenatal vitamins should include folic acid to meet your increased requirement.

Emotional Changes

Most women find the second trimester to be a more positive experience than the first, as they are now beginning to feel the movements of the life within them. Most husbands by now have accepted the existence of the pregnancy and are as excited as the woman about the movements of the baby. During this trimester, men frequently also become more aware of their wife's growing dependence on them. As the pregnancy progresses, the woman may feel more vulnerable and may need her mate's attention more. She may want him to become more involved with the pregnancy and the baby. In addition, she may become overly concerned for her husband's safety. Meanwhile, the husband may share the woman's interest in the pregnancy, or he may feel an increased creative interest in his work or hobby. He may gain weight or show other symptoms of pregnancy. These are all ways in which expectant mothers and fathers deal with the stresses and changes that are occurring. It is important for both partners to be aware of and to talk about their feelings, especially when friction arises between them.

A woman's dreams may become very real during this trimester and are sometimes disturbing. Dreams are a way of bringing fears to consciousness, where they can be dealt with more easily. Dreaming about misfortune to the baby or to herself, or about giving birth to animals is common. If a woman refuses to acknowledge her fears, she may suffer increasing anxiety.

THIRD TRIMESTER

The third trimester of pregnancy is the last 3 months, or from the twenty-ninth through the fortieth week of gestation. It is a time of preparing for the birth, physically, mentally, and emotionally.

Physical Changes

The major physical changes that women experience during the third trimester include the following:

Uterus : Toward the end of pregnancy, the uterus reaches the breastbone, or sternum, and measures about 11 by 14 inches. Lightening occurs from 1 to 6 weeks before delivery. This means that the baby's head settles downward into the pelvis and may engage in the pelvic inlet.

Braxton-Hicks contractions become stronger and more apparent as the time for delivery approaches. The cervix becomes softer during the last few weeks and may begin to thin out and open up a little in preparation for labor. The woman may feel a sharp pain in thc groin if she moves suddenly. This pain is caused by a spasm in or stretching of the round ligaments. These ligaments are a main support of the uterus and extend into the groin area on both sides.

Vagina : As the pregnancy nears its end, more mucus is passed vaginally in preparation for the baby's passage. The vaginal swelling also increases at this time and may result in discomfort during sexual intercourse.

Digestion : The growing uterus puts pressure on the stomach and intestines, pushing them up and back. Heartburn, a burning sensation felt in the chest, may occur. This is caused by the escape of gastric contents into the esophagus as a result of the relaxation of the sphincter at the top of the stomach. Problems with constipation may continue.

Breathing : Shortness of breath is common because the uterus is pushing upon the diaphragm. This improves after lightening. Many women also experience nasal congestion and may even have nosebleeds.

Vision : Some women experience a change in vision, possibly requiring new glasses or preventing them from wearing their contacts. Report any change in vision to your caregiver, since it may be the result of gestational diabetes, pregnancy-induced hypertension or another serious problem.

Circulation : Varicose veins may develop in the legs, vulva, or rectum (hemorrhoids). Varicose veins are caused by the increased pelvic pressure exerted by the uterus and growing fetus, as well as by the decrease in blood returned from the lower body and limbs. They usually diminish after delivery.

Urination : The need to urinate usually increases, especially after lightening occurs. This is caused by the pressure of the baby on the bladder.

Fatigue : Carrying around the extra weight causes fatigue to return during the last trimester.

Emotional Changes

During the third trimester, most women focus more and more on the baby and on labor and delivery. Both parents-to-be find that the search for the perfect name has become an important pastime. They also spend time preparing an area in the house for the baby. Almost all women by now have accepted that they are pregnant and are able to differentiate their babies as real people, separate from themselves.

Time during the third trimester seems endless. Many women count on their due date to bring the end of their discomfort and may be very discouraged if they go a week or more beyond.

Because of their large size, some women experience a drop in self-esteem during this trimester. They need the people around them, especially their husbands, to reassure them that they are still attractive.

You can use your preoccupation with labor and delivery to your advantage at this time. Gather as much information about the birth experience as possible. Read books, take classes and talk to new mothers. However, avoid people who repeatedly attempt to discourage you from taking prepared childbirth classes or who dwell on negative birth experiences. You need to keep a confident, relaxed attitude toward the upcoming event. Do not avoid your fears, but at the same time, do not allow negative thinking to dominate you. Your chances for a positive birth experience are to a great extent determined by your attitude. Fear and anxiety create negative experiences.

Infertility Problem ? When to Start Worrying

Before beginning to get worried, one should remember that, in a single menstrual cycle, the chance of a perfectly normal couple achieving a successful pregnancy is only about 25%, even if they have sex every single day. This is called their fecundity, which describes their fertility potential. Despite the phenomenal population growth, it should be emphasized that humans are not very efficient at producing babies ! There are many reasons for this, including the fact that some eggs don't fertilize and some of the fertilized eggs don't grow well in the early developmental stage. Getting pregnant is a game of odds—it's a bit like playing Russian roulette. It's impossible to predict when an individual couple will succeed in achieving pregnancy ! However, over a period of one year, the chance of achieving a successful pregnancy is between 80% and 90% ; in other words, 7 out of 8 couples will be on their way to becoming parents within a year. These are the normal "fertile" couples and the rest are labelled "infertile"; the medical textbook definition of infertility being "the inability to conceive even after trying for one year". Couples who have never had a child are said to have "primary infertility"; those women who have become pregnant at least once but are unable to conceive again, are said to have "secondary infertility".

The chances of achieving pregnancy for a couple in a given cycle will depend upon many factors, and the most important ones are :

- The age of the woman. As the biological clock ticks on, the number of eggs and their quality starts decreasing.
- Frequency of intercourse. While there is no "normal" frequency for sex, the "optimal" frequency of intercourse (if the woman is trying to get pregnant) is about 3 times a week during the fertile period. Simply stated, the more sex the better ! Couples who have intercourse less frequently have a diminished chance of conceiving.
- "Trying time", that is, how long the couple have been trying to get pregnant. This is an important concept. The longer a couple has been trying to conceive without success, the lesser their chances of getting pregnant without medical help.
- The presence of fertility problems.

What happens when a couple has an infertility problem ? The chances of the wife getting pregnant depends upon a number of variables multiplied together. Let us consider a hypothetical example where both the husband and the wife have a condition that impairs their fertility. The wife has a condition that impairs their fertility. The husband's fertility, based on a reduced sperm count, is 50% of the normal value. His wife ovulates only in 50% of cycles; and one of her fallopian tubes is blocked. With 3 relative infertility factors, the chance of conception is calculated as follows : 0.5 (sperm count) x 0.5 (ovulation factor) x 0.5 (tubal factor) = 0.125, or 12.5% of normal. Since the chance of conception in normal fertile couples is only 25% in any one cycle, the probability of pregnancy in any given month for this couple, without treatment is only about 3% (0.125 x 25 = 0.03125) ! Even if they kept on trying for 5 years, the chance of conceiving on their own would be 60% only. Thus, infertility problems multiply together and magnify the odds against a couple achieving a pregnancy. This is why it is important to correct or improve each partner's contributing infertility factors as much as possible in order to maximize the chances of conception.

If infertile couples had 300 years in which to breed, most wives would get pregnant without any treatment at all ! Of course, time is at a premium, so the odds need to be improved—and this is where medical treatment comes in.

When should you seek medical advice ?

If you have been having sexual intercourse two or three times a week at about the time of ovulation, without any form of birth control for a year or more and have not become pregnant, you meet the definition of being infertile. Pregnancy may still occur spontaneously, but from a statistical point of view, the chances are decreasing and you may now want to start thinking about seeking medical help. There is no precise "right" time to do so, and if it is causing you anxiety and worry, then you should consult a doctor. Even though you may be embarrassed and feel that you are the only ones in the world facing this problem, you should not forget that you are not alone. Many couples experience infertility and many can be helped.

A note of caution should be sounded at this stage.

There are certain conditions that warrant seeing a doctor sooner;

- Period occurring at three-week (or less) intervals.
- Periods not occuring for longer than three months.
- Irregular periods.
- A history of pelvic infection.
- Two or more miscarriages.
- Women over the age of 35 — time is not at a premium !
- Men who have had prostate infections.
- Men whose testes are not felt in the scrotum.

Tips for Self-help

Before seeking medical help, remember some of the things you can do to enhance your own fertility potential.

Body weight, diet and exercise : Proper diet and exercise are important for optimal reproductive function. Women who are significantly overweight or underweight can face difficulties in getting pregnant. Consult you doctor about a healthy diet. Normal exercise, including aerobics, tennis or jogging, may improve your chance of conceiving; However excessive exercise (for example, jogging over three miles per day) can adversely affect your valuation.

Stop smoking : In men, cigarette smoking has been associated with a decreased sperm count. Women who smoke take longer to conceive.

Stop drinking alcohol : Alcohol (beer and wine as well as hard liquor) intake in men has been associated with a low sperm count.

Review your medications : A number of medications, including some of these used to treat ulcer problems and high blood pressure, can influence a man's sperm count. If you are taking any medications, have a talk with your doctor about whether or not such medication can affect your fertility.

Many medications taken during early pregnancy can affect the foetus. It is important to inform your doctor that you are attempting to become pregnant before taking prescription medications or over-the-counter medications, such as aspirin, antihistamines, or diet pills.

Stop abusing drugs : Drugs such as marijuana and anabolic steroids decrease sperm counts. If you have used drugs, discuss this aspect with your doctor. This is confidential information. Both partners should stop using any illicit drugs if they want a healthy baby. Also, limit your caffeine (tea, soft drinks and coffee) intake.

Frequency of intercourse : The simple rule is : as often as you like; the more often you have sex, the better your chances. Thus, for couples who have sex only on weekends (often the price they pay for a heavy work schedule) the chance of having sex on the fertile prevulatory day is only one-third that of couples who have sex every other day. This means they (the "weekends") may take three times as long to conceive.

Timing of intercourse : Unlike animals, who know instinctively when to have sex in order to conceive (because the female is in "heat" or when she ovulates), most couples have no idea when the woman ovulates. Timing the intercourse during the "fertile period" is important and can be easily learnt. However, some couples are so anxious about having sex at exactly the right time that they may abstain for a whole week prior to the "evaluator day" — and often the doctor is the culprit in this over-igorous scheduling of sex. Such overattention can be counter-productive (because of the anxiety and stress it generates) and is not advisable.

Position and technique of intercourse : A very interesting fact of nature is that pigs are very efficient at conserving semen — the boar literally screws his penis into the vagina of the sow, obtaining a tight lock prior to ejaculation, to ensure that no semen leaks out. Humans do not have such well-designed mechanisms of technique; perhaps this is because they are really not necessary. Most doctors advise a male superior position and also advise that the woman remain lying down for at least 5 minutes after sex and not wash or douche afterwards. A number of products used for lubrication during intercourse, such as petroleum jelly or vaginal cream, have been shown to affect sperm quality. Therefore, these products should be avoided if you are trying to get pregnant (a suitable alternative is raw egg white).

Is Fertility Lower at Present ?

Has the fertility of couples declined in modern times ? Possibly. The reasons for this downfall include the following :

1. The increasing age of women at the time of marriage and child bearing.
2. The increased incidence of sexually transmitted diseases (STDs) which damage the reproductive tract in both men and women.

3. Decreasing sperm counts in men which is a global phenomenon. An interesting observation made recently has been that men's sperm counts worldwide have been falling in the last few decades. Whether this pehnomenon is due to environmental pollution, or due to the stresses of modern day life, remains unclear.

Where to Get Help

Most couples usually consult their family physician, who will refer them to an obstetrician-gynecologist when infertility poses problems. This first visit should include both partners. The physician will usually outline the possible causes of infertility and provide an evaluation plan. The first step should be to achieve an accurate diagnosis to try to find out why pregnancy isn't occurring. Once a diagnosis has been determined, the couple and physician should meet again and chalk out a treatment plan. For difficult and complex problems, an infertility specialist should be consulted.

Artificial Insemination/Test Tube Babies and Surrogate Mothering

Artificial insemination by husband (AIH) is useful in the following cases :

1. The woman has a cervical mucus problem. For example, the mucus may be scanty or hostile to the sperm. With an intrauterine insemination (IUI), the sperm can bypass her cervix and enter the uterine cavity directly.
2. The man has antibodies to this own sperm. The "good" sperm which have not been affected by the antibodies are separated in the laboratory and used for IUI.
3. If the man cannot ejaculate into his partner's vagina. This situation arises because of psychological problems such as impotence (inability to get and maintain an erection) and vaginismus (an involuntary spasm of the vaginal muscles so that vaginal penetration is not possible); or because of anatomic problems of the penis, such as uncorrected hypospadias; or if the man is paraplegic.
4. The man suffers from retrograde ejaculation in which the semen goes backward into the bladder instead of coming out of the penis.
5. For unexplained infertility, since the technique of IUI increases the chances of the eggs and sperm meeting.

6. As an inexpensive alternative to GIFT, IUI is a reasonable first choice (especially for younger couples) since it is so much cheaper and less intrusive.
7. If the husband is away from the wife for long stretches of time (for example, husband who work on ships or work aboard), his sperm can be frozen and stored in a sperm bank and used to inseminate his wife even in his absence.
8. For male factor infertility, though this is a controversial area, especially for the common problem of oligospermia (a low sperm count). What is the rationale behind using IUI for treating this problem ? Remember that infertility is a problem of the couple's, not just the oligospermic male's. Whether a given couple will conceive or not depends on the sum of their fertility potential of the wife is improved by superovulating her, so that instead of producing just one egg per cycle, she produced 2-4 eggs per cycle. In addition, the husband's sperm are processed in the laboratory, and the best sperm are used for IUI. This increases the chances of the best sperm being able to reach and fertilize the egg.

Test Tube Babies - IVF and GIFT

IVF

IVF is a method of assisted reproduction in which the man's sperm and the woman's egg are combined in a laboratory dish, where fertilization occurs. The resulting embryo is transferred to the woman's uterus. The basic steps in an IVF treatment cycle are ovulation enhancement (stimulating the development of more than one egg in a cycle), egg harvest, fertilization, embryo culture and embryo transfer.

IVF can be a reasonable treatment choice for couples with various types of infertility. Initially, it was only used when the woman had blocked, damaged, or absent fallopian tubes (tubal factor infertility). IVF is now also used to circumvent infertility caused by endometroiosis, immunological problems, unexplained infertility, and male factor infertility.

GIFT

GIFT stands for gamete intrafallopian transfer. A gamete is a male or female sex cell—a sperm or an egg. During GIFT, sperm and eggs are mixed and injected into one or both fallopian tubes. After the gametes have been transferred, fertilization can take place in the fallopian tube as it does in natural, unassisted reproduction. Once fertilized, the embryo travels to the uterus by natural processes.

As in IVF, a GIFT treatment cycle begins with ovulation enhancement which is followed by egg harvest, usually by means of laparoscopy. But the similarity to IVF ends here. In IVF, an embryo is transferred. In GIFT, only gametes are transferred.

Only patients who have at least one normal, healthy fallopian tube are candidates for GIFT. Such patients include women who have unexplained infertility or mild endometrosis and couples whose infertility results from male, cervical, or immunological factors. Some doctors recommend that couples with male factor infertility proceed with GIFT only if it has been proven that the man's sperm can fertilize the woman's egg either by in vitro fertilization or by past pregnancies.

Surrogate Mothering

The word "SURROGATE" means substitute or replacement and a surrogate mother is one who lends her uterus to another couple so that they can have a baby. In the West where fewer and fewer babies are offered for adoption, surrogacy is gaining popularity, despite controversial legal and ethical hassles.

Which kinds of women need surrogates ? The commonest reason is a woman who has no uterus. The uterus may be absent from birth (Mullerian agencies); or may have been removed surgically (hysterectomy for life-saving reasons, such as excessive bleeding during a Caesarean section operation). Other women have suffered to explore surrogacy include those who have suffered multiple miscarriages or who have failed to conceive despite repeated attempts at IVF for unexplained reasons.

Women who agree to become surrogates may do so for compassionate reasons. Such women could include a sister, mother or a close friend of the couple. They may also do so for financial remuneration, and this could be a woman, with or without children, known or unknown to the couple, who "rents" out her womb for a fee.

There are two main kinds of surrogacy :

1. The surrogate mother provides the egg. In this case, the surrogate is inseminated artificially by the husband's sperm. Thus, the infertile woman has no genetic relationship to the baby.
2. More commonly, the infertile woman provides the eggs, which are then either transferred along with her husband's sperm to the surrogate mother's fallopian tubes by GIFT, or they are fertilized in vitro by IVF with her husband's sperm and the resulting embryos are then transferred to the surrogate's uterus, which then acts as an incubator for the next nine months.

Certain guidelines have been laid down in order to try to minimize misuse of the surrogacy technique and a surrogate motherhood contract needs to be drawn up, which should specify that the child will become the legitimate adopted child of the infertile couple, i.e., the intended parents. This contract needs to be signed by the couple, the surrogate, and her husband (if any), but cannot be held to the legally binding.

The "legal waters" of surrogate motherhood will continue to be murky, and, at present, no laws or guidelines exist in India. This is why the element of trust between the couple and the surrogate mother is so important.

It is vital that the surrogate and the couple consider

the future of the child. The receiving mother should ideally be present at the birth and care for the baby in hospital. She can even be prepared for breast feeding by hormone treatment (induced lactation).

Surrogacy has spawned a host of legal and emotional questions to which there are no right answers. For example :

- What will you do if the surrogate insists on keeping the child ?
- How much should you pay the surrogate ?
- If the surrogate becomes seriously ill as a result of the pregnancy, who will pay the medical costs ?
- Is it possible to put the receiving mother's name as the "mother" on the child's birth certificate ?
- Will you steal the child after the surrogacy ?
- Will surrogates undertake pregnancy merely for profit ?
- What happens if the child is handicapped and is unwanted by the couple and the surrogate mother ?
- What happens if the surrogate dies during child birth ?

Many people are worried about the possibility of the surrogacy technique being misused. They feel it may allow the exploitation of poor women who may be used as "mother machines" to bear babies, much like the wet nurses of yesteryears.

Surrogacy has received quite a lot of adverse press publicity recently, especially when the contract goes sour and there is a dispute over the baby between the commissioning parents and the surrogate mother. Such a situation makes headline news. The courts then need to have the wisdom of Solomon to assign the rights of the "genetic" mother; the "birth" mother; and the "social or rearing" mother.

Nevertheless, we must remember that surrogacy does offer one method of achieving parenthood to a few couples who could never possibly have a baby by any other means.

What to do for Good Birth Experience

What	Why ?
Optimum nutrition	The No-Risk Pregnancy Diet can reduce the danger of complications for you and your baby to the lowest possible level.
Supportive care giver willing to be flexible in your labor and delivery choices, including birth place (hospital or birth center)	Careful selection of your care giver can eliminate the stress of trying to change the attitudes of a doctor or midwife who will not consider your individual wishes. Some low-risk women feel more at home in an out-of-hospital birth centre. Others feel safer within a hospital environment.
Consumer-oriented childbirth classes	Consumer-oriented classes inform you about all the available options rather than just the routine of a particular hospital or doctor. They enable you to make educated decisions about what options you want for your childbirth experience, plus provide you with thorough training for labor and delivery.
No smoking, taking drugs, or consuming alcohol	These have been shown by experts to have adverse effects on the baby.
No routine use of ultrasound during pregnacy	Routine screening of all women is not recommended by the Obstetricians and Gyneaecologists.

	DURING LABOR
Presence of a support person during the admission procedures, examination, labor and birth.	This eliminates the stress of seperation. Your partner can provide emotional support during labor and birth, as well as during any necessary procedures. His presence can enhance family bonding.
Presence of other family members or friends during labor and / or delivery.	Other family members and friends can provide additional support for you and your partner.
Enema only if needed	The incidence of infection does not increase as long as those patients have no signs of illness (for example, runny nose or diarrhea).
Freedom to move about and to assume a position of comfort	Walking stimulates the uterus to work more efficiently. Labors that include walking are documented to be shorter and to require less pain medication. Sitting up, lying on your side, or kneeling on your hands and knees may be most comfortable for you.
Laboring in water	Laboring in a tub or shower enhances relaxation and decreases the need for pain medicationa.

Liquid nourishment and high-carbohydrate, low-fat snacks as desired	Foods that are high in carbohydrates and low in fat are digested quickly and supply energy that will be needed during labor. Liquids prevent dehydration.
Ice chips, sips of water or clear juice.	Your mouth can become very dry when you do the breathing patterns.
Personal items (for example, night-gown, music, or flowers)	Familiar articles can enhance your birth experience by encouraging relaxation and comfort.
Prep (shaving of the pubic hair) only if desired.	Shaving of the pubic hair does not decrease the incidence of infection, and the regrowth of the hair is uncomfortable.
Intravenous (IV) fluids only if medically indicated.	IVS restrict mobility and interfere with relxation. Clear liquids during labor reduce the chance of dehydrataion. Hemorrhage is rare when the birth is unmedicated and spontaneous, and when breastfeeding is begun immediately.
Electronic fetal monitor only if medically indicated.	In a low-risk woman, a trained nurse frequently listening to the fetal heart rate has been shown to be as effective in detecting fetal well-being or distress as an electronic fetal monitor. Fetal monitors restrict movement and can be uncomfortable. Sometimes, women are instructed to lie on their backs, a position

	that can be uncomfortable and can also negatively affect labor. Intermittent use of a fetal monitor throughout labor is alternative.
Spontaneous rupture of the membranes	The amniotic fluid contained in the membranes has a cushioning effect, equalizing the pressure on the baby, which result in less molding of his head. Artificial ruputre of the membranes provide a passage way for infection and creates a time limit for delivery.
Medication administered only when requested by you and with full information regarding the possible effect on you, the baby, and the labor	All medication has the potential to affect you, your baby and your labor. Knowledge of the benefits and risks of the medications your care giver uses most often will enable you to make informed decisions.
Presence of a professional labor support person (childbirth instructor, registered nurse, trained doula, licensed massage therapist, or midwife not associated with the hospital or birth center).	A knowledgeable professional who has a strong commitment to the type of birth you desire can provide you with additional information. The presence of a doula can reduce your chances of having a cesarean by 50 percent. Also, your labor may be shorter, you may require less Pitocin and pain medication, and you may reduce your needs for an epidural and a forceps delivery. A massage theraptist can perform techniques to relieve labor *discomfort*.

Pitocin to induce or augment labor only if medically indicated	The contractions induced by Pitocin are more difficult to handle than natural contractiions for both the woman and baby. The risks of induced labor include reduction of the baby's oxygen supply and premature birth, which are not warranted just for the woman's or doctor's convenience (elective induction). The complications that may develop in a labor involving Pitocin can increase the chances for cesarean delivery.
DURING DELIVERY	
Comfortable and effecient pushing and delivery position	Semireclining at a 70-degree angle, side-lying, or kneeling may be more comfortable than being flat on your back. Lying flat on your back reduces the pelvic outlet to its smallest diameter, may be uncomortable and causes the weight of the uterus to impede blood flow. Squatting shortens the birth canal, opens the pelvic outlet to its widest diameter, and makes the contractions more efficient because the uterus is assisted by *gravity*.
No use of stirrups	The lithotomy position, in which you lie on your back with your feet in stirrups, works against gravity and forces you to push the baby uphills. Wide stirrups, while giving the care giver a good field of vision, cause the perineum to be stretched and increase the need for an episiotomy (a small incision in the vaginal outlet to enlarge the opening).

Episiotomy only if needed	Allowing the baby's head to emerge slowly under uterine force alone gives the parineal tissue a better chance to stretch, which minimizes tearing. An episiotomy shortens the pushing stage. It may be necessary if fetal distress is detected and a faster delivery or the use of forceps is required. Many doctors do an episiotomy may be very uncomfortable. Muscle scarring, which can negatively affect later sexual pleasure, can result.
Use of a birthing room or the same bed for labor and delivery	This avoids the stress and discomfort of being rushed to a delivery room during the expulsion stage and of then being awkwardly moved onto a delivery table. Most hospitals do provide birthing rooms for labour and delivery.
Regional anesthesia only if medical or surgical intervention becomes necessary.	Anesthesia is unnecessary in an uncomplicated delivery. If an episiotomy is done, a local anesthetic may be given for repair work after the baby is delivered. Regional anesthesia is compatible with an awake delivery; general anesthesia is not.
Leboyer delivery (gentle birth)	Gentle birth is an attitude as well as a procedure. It decreases the sensory and physical trauma to the infant as he is delivered.
Cutting the cord delayed until the pulsating stops.	The delay allows the baby to continue receiving oxygen through the cord while his respiratory system begins to functions.

Father cutting the umbilican cord	This increases his participation in the birth.
Collection of cord blood for banking	Collection of cord blood for donation or for storage for your own personal use may provide lifesaving benefits.
Baby placed immediately on your bare abdomen or in your arms	Immediate skin-to-skin contact is beneficial. When both mother and baby are covered with a blanket, the infant's temperature can be maintained.
Antibiotic ointment or silver nitrate drops delayed until after bonding	The baby's sucking stimulates the mother's production of the hormone oxytocin, which aids in the release of the placenta and decreases postpartum bleeding. A baby's sucking reflex is strongest during the first hours after birth. Colostrum (the first milk produced in the breasts) acts as a laxative, cleanising the baby's intestinal tract of mucus and meconium (fetal fecal matter).
Antibiotic ointment or silver nitrate drops delayed until after bonding	These can interfere with the baby's vision, which is so important during the bonding period.
Placenta allowed to detach spontaneously from the wall of the uterus	Strong traction or massaging may cause placental tissue to be retained, which can cause postpartum bleeding.

Bonding	The first hours after birth are very important in the development of maternal and paternal attachment to the newborn.
Taking snapshots or making a tape	These are wonderful ways to remember these unforgettable moments.
Breastfeeding	Nutritionally, your breastmilk is the perfect food for your baby. Breastfeeding is an emotinally satisfying experience for both mother and baby. It is economical. It helps the uterus return to its prepregnant state faster.
No seperation of mother and baby unless medically indicated.	Continuous mother-baby contact enhances bonding. It also increases the opportunity for the nurse to provide baby-care instruction. The initial bath can be given in the mother's room.
No supplements (water or formula) or pacifiers if breastfeeding.	Sucking on a rubber nipple may confuse your baby, since he must use a different tongue action to suck from your breast. If your baby is fed supplements between nursings, he may not breastfeed as often as necessary to stimulate milk production.
Full 24-hours rooming in	This allows close contact between parents and baby to enhacne the bonding process, depending on the mother's postpartum condition.

	You are able to breastfeed on demand. You can learn how to care for your baby while supervised by hospital staff. This enhances family bonding.
Father staying in the room with the mother until discharge	It enables the father to assist with the baby care. Many hospitals provide cots for fathers to spend the night. This helps reassure your other children that you are fine.
Sibling visiting with mother and baby	It encourages acceptance of the new baby by his siblings.
Circumcision only if desired	Circumcisions is normally done for religious or cosmetic reasons. It should be delayed for 12 to 24 hours after birth to give the baby time to adjust to extrauterine life. It may cause bleeding or infection.
Discharge from the hospital within 24 hours after birth.	This decreases the chances of a hospital-induced infection. Early discharge is safe as long as there is adequate follow-up care for the mother and baby. The decision should be made on an individual basis. It decreases the time you are seperated from your other children.

When to Avoid Sex During Pregnancy

You should avoid sex during pregnancy:

- *If you are at risk for preterm labor.*
- *If you have a placenta previa (low-lying placenta).*
- *If you have an incompetent cervix.*
- *If you experience vaginal bleeding.*
- *If your membranes have ruptured or you are leaking fluid.*
- *If you have an active herpes lesion.*
- *If you experience pain with intercourse.*
- *If you have a vaginal infection or an undiagnosed vaginal discharge.*

Your caregiver will advise you in this area!

Care During Delivery

It is important that delivery is always conducted by a trained health worker only.

The health worker will take necessary precautions to ensure that you give birth to a healthy child and your health is also protected.

You should know that if a delivery is conducted by an untrained person, (e.g. untrained local *dai*), chances of complications like excessive bleeding and infection to you and the newborn are much more. Many mothers die in India every year due to such happenings.

A trained health worker will carefully ensure the following "cleans" during a delivery

To facilitate the work of a trained health worker, it is advisable that you keep the following items in readiness before delivery:

- Clean, washed pieces of clothes and sheets
- A brand new blade/razor
- Clean thread
- Soap and towel

A clean room for delivery is also to be kept ready.

The blade/knife or the razor and the thread used to tie the umbilical cord should be made germ free by boiling them in water for atleast 20 minutes.

If somehow it is not possible for the delivery to be conducted by a trained health worker and the local untrained *dai* has to be called, make sure that :

- The *dai* washes her hands thoroughly with soap and water.
- She uses only a blade/knife and the string which have been made germ free by boiling.

Don't even apply cow dung. ghee or any such items on the umbilical cord stump on child's abdomen. These can cause infection of the umbilical cord and thus can be dangerous.

It is good to remember that most of the deliveries don't require to be conducted in a hospital. Home deliveries are as safe and good if conducted by a trained health worker. Yes, "High Risk Mothers" need to deliver in a hospital only. As mentioned earlier also, your family members must ensure that a fast transport is readily available which may be required to transport you to a nearby hospital in case a problem arises during delivery.

Care of the child in first 24 hours after birth

Every new-born child—whether girl or boy—is like a lovely, delicate flower. Moreover, the child is absolutely helpless and completely at your mercy. Such a flower needs your tender, loving, right kind of care and attention.

Remember the following :

1. Record the birth weight of the child. This will tell you whether the baby is of normal weight or not. (Indian children with 2.8kg. birth weight are considered to be a of normal weight.) Birth weight will be of use even in future. A baby with birth weight less than 2.5 kg. is a low birth weight baby. Such a baby is at a greater risk of developing various health problems.

2. Breast feeding : Put your newborn to breast within the first hour after delivery. Breast milk is extremely important for proper growth and development of the child.

The initial thick, yellowish milk, called colostrum, is very good for the baby and must never be discarded. Feed colostrum to the baby. It is a very vital food: rich in disease preventing substances and hence extremely important for your newborn. Many mothers who do not know this, discard the colostrum. Never do that.

Do not give anything else to the child. Many a mother give. sugar solution ghutti, honey, etc. to the newborn. They are not required and, infact, can be dangerous.

The baby gets plenty of water in breast milk and hence even water should not be given to the baby—not even in hot, summer months. Look at baby's lips and mouth for dryness. Increase the feeds accordingly.

Always wash both your breasts properly before breast feeding. This helps in prevention of infections being transmitted to the child.

It is also advised to use both the breasts for feeding in one sitting . Always sit, hold the baby correctly and then breast-fed. Follow this rule even for night feeds.

Remember, breast milk is the best for your most precious possession, i.e., your baby.

Continue breastfeeding as long as you can.

3. Get your new-born immunized with BCG if the child has been delivered in a hospital. Also give a dose of Oral Polio Vaccine (OPV). Don't apply anything on the umbilical cord stump on the baby's abdomen. just keep it clean and dry.

5. In winter months, keep the child sufficiently warm by adequate clothing.

6. If the child becomes blue/develops any other problem/ does not suck well, please consult a health worker immediately.

Diet for the Pregnant Woman

The diet of the pregnant lady could be balanced and free of oils, spices, junk food.

Breakfast

Fruits, fruit juice, sprouted pulses, lean meats, fresh boiled eggs, cheese, bread or a slice or toast with butter, milk, tea or coffee.

She may select a few items from the above mentioned list.

Mid-day meal

Rice, dal (pulse-soup) cooked or raw vegetables, chappatis, bread, milk, fruits, meats, curds, eggs, fish, cheese, chicken, mineral waters, etc.

(*She may select four or five items from above*).

Dinner

Khichadi, vegetable-broth, bread, milk, fruits, bean, meats, egg, fish, cheese, chicken, white meats etc.

(*She may select four or five items from above*)

She must be cautious to take the above mentioned items in as much quantity as neither make her feel starved or overfed. She may also take appropriate amounts of milk, dry fruits, fresh fruits, curds or biscuit if she really feels hungry. It may be recalled that it is better to consume less food with greater frequency than to have large amounts with long intervals. Besides, she must be cautious as to not become obese which might create more problems not only for her but also for the child.

During pregnancy, the normal daily intake of food should be following.

About 250 gms. of flour, 100 gms. of dal, 1 kg milk, ghee or oil 50 to 60 gms; sugar 20 gms, fresh fruits 1 or 2, lean meats 20 gms, eggs-4, green vegetables 200-250 gms.

This diet would give her about 2600 to 2800 calories with all the necessary nutrients.

Table Showing Calories of Different Foods

	Food	Calories
1.	*Cereals*	
	Wheat	346
	Wheat flour	341
	Maida (refined wheat flour)	348
	Bajra (pearl millets)	361
	Banti	371
	Rice	346
	Maize	342
	Jowar(sorghum, milo)	349
	jav (barley)	336
	Ragi (ginger millets)	328
	Sooji (rava, semolina)	348
2.	*Pulses and Legumes*	
	Chana dal (split bengal grams)	372
	Bhuna chana (roasted Bengal grams)	369
	Chana flour (Bengal gram flour)	360
	Moong (green grams)	348
	Moong dal (split green grams)	347
	Urad dal (split black grams)	347
	masoor dal (split lentils)	343

3.	**Peas**	323
	Tuver (pigeon peas, red grams)	335
	Soya-beans	432
4.	***Roots and Tubers***	
	Carrots	48
	Potatoes	97
	Potato chips	500
	Sweet potatoes	79
	Onions	50
	Beet roots	43
	Aravi (arum, colocasia) tubers	56
5.	***Vegetables, Spices and Condiments***	
	Karela (bitter gourd)	25
	Kankods (momordica)	52
	Dudhi (bottle gourd)	12
	Brinjals (baigan, egg plant)	24
	Valpapadi (Field bean, hyacinth bean pods)	85
	Cauliflower	57
	Gavar (cluster bean pods)	16
	Pea pods	93
	Cucumber	13
	Saragavo (drumsticks)	26
	Bhindi (Bhinda, ladies fingers, okra)	35
	Cabbage	27
	Turia (torai, ridge gourd)	17
	Tomatoes	20
	Phanasi (French beans)	26
	Aravi (arum colocasia) leaves	56
	Methi (fenugreek)	49
	Radish (mula, muli)	28
	Palak (spinach)	26
	Tindola (Tinda)	21
	Green chillies	29
	Garlic saplings	67
	Garlic (dried)	145
	Chilli powder	246
	Turmeric	349

6. *Fruits*

Rayon	134
Amla (myrobalan, Indian gooseberry)	58
Seetaphal (custard apple, sugar apple)	104
Apple	59
Banana	116
Raspberries	56
Strawberries	44
Guavas	51
Jack fruit	88
Jamuns (rose apples, Jamun fruit)	62
Lemons	50
Mango	80
Alphonso mango	120
Watermelon	16
Orange	72
Mosambi (sweet lime)	48
Papaya	43
Pineapple	32
Grapes	58
Chiku (sapota)	94

7. *Dry Fruits*

Almonds (10 to 12 nuts)	600
Cashewnuts (6 to 8 nuts)	88
Cashewnuts(100 gramms)	596
Figs	37
Walnuts	687
Coconut	444
Dried coconut kernel	334
Dates	317

8. *Milk, Milk Preparations, and Other Sweets*

Buffalo's milk	117
Cow's milk	67
Ewe's milk	72
Skimmed milk	70
Human milk	65
Milk powder	350 to 500

Curds	60
Curds (without cream)	55
Butter	729
Ghee (clarified butter)	900
Cheese	348
Kheer	176
Mattha	265
Khoya	417
Ice-cream	200 to 300
Milk cake	331
Custard (cooked)	114
Shreekhand	250
Pista barfi	950
Kaju barfi	950
Copra pak	950
Mysore pak	950
Ras malai	950
Badam halva	570
Milk halva	950
Sown halva (sohan halva)	950
Rabadi (basoodi)	1200
Sooji kheer	600
Nan khatai	584
Jalebi	400
Rasagulla	600
9. ***Animal Foods***	
Whole flesh	194
Mutton	118
Goat's meat	118
Pork	114
Beef	410
Liver	194
Chicken	70
Fish	87
Eggs	173
One egg (=50 gramms)	86
Yolk of egg	68

	White of egg	13
	Omelette	108
10.	***Sweetening Agents***	
	Gur (jaggery) (1 tablespoonful, 15 gramms)	57
	sugar (1 teaspoonful, 5 grammes)	20
	Sugar (1 cube)	12
	Unrefined sugar (1 tablespoonful, 15 gramms)	45
11.	***Fats and Oils***	
	Processed butter	755
	Cream	213
	Ghee, fat, any vegetable oil (e.g. groundnut oil, sunflower oil, cotton seed oil), Vegetable ghee (all are similar in calories, composition, differing only in proportions of various fatty acids	900
	Margarine (sunbeam)	755
12.	***Other Foods, Generally Served as Snacks***	
	Saada Dosa(1)	100
	Masala Dosa (1)	250
	Sambar (1 cup)	210
	Idli(3)	200
	Thick dal (1 cup)	145
	Thick watery dal (1 cup)	145
	Thin watery dal (1 cup)	92
	small puri (1)	150
	Patties (1)	150
	Pani puri (1 plate)	125
	Bhel puri (1 cup)	280
	Papadi (1 plate)	25
	Dhokla (1 cup)	122
	Pakoras (1 plate)	200
	Kachauri (40 gramms)	200
	Potato chips (60 gramms)	200
	Chana (cooked) (30 gramms)	200
	Samosa (70 grammes)	200
	Dahi wada (30 gramms)	200
	Chaat (1 plate)	474
	Sev (1 plate)	550

	Chakri (1 plate)	550
	Chivda(1 plate)	420
13.	***Drinks and Beverages***	
	Apple juice (200 ml)	95
	Coconut water (200 ml)	50
	Cola (1 bottle)	80
	Tea (without sugar, with 1 oz milk) (1 cup)	25
	Coffee (without sugar, with 1 oz milk) (1 cup)	25
	Grape juice (200 ml)	65
	Limca (1 bottle)	50
	Orange juice (200 ml)	95
	Tomato juice (200 ml)	45
	Beer (240 ml)	112
	Brandy (1 peg) (30 ml)	73
	Rum (43 ml)	105
	Whisky (43)	105
	Sherry (60 ml)	84
	Sweet wine (port) (100 ml)	160
	Horlicks (2 teaspoonful)	41
	Ovaltine (2 teaspoonful)	35
	Bournvita (2 teaspoonful)	35

1 Teaspoon (small spoon) Contains about 5 ml, 5 gms.
1 Tableshpoon (large spoon) contains about, 15 ml, 15gms
1 Cup (large spoon) contains about 150 ml, 150gms.

Note : In the table, unit is per 100 gms. unless indicated otherwise.

Breast Feeding

Breast-milk contains all essential nutrients needed for the infant; it provides the best nutrition and protects the infant from infections. Breast-milk is a natural food and is more easily digested and absorbed by the infant as compared to formula milk prepared from other sources. Colostrum, which is the milk secreted during the first 3 days after child birth, is rich in proteins, minerals, vitamins especially vitamin A and antibodies. In addition, it has a laxative effect as well. Breast-feeding helps in reducing fertility and facilitates spacing of children. Lactation provides emotional satisfaction to the mother and the infant. Therefore, breast milk is the best milk for the newborn and growing infant.

What are the advantages of breast-milk ?

In addition to providing nutrients, breast-milk has several special components such as growth factors, enzymes, hormones and anti-infective factors. The amount of milk secreted increases gradually in the first few days after delivery, reaching the peak during the second month, at which level it is maintained until about 4-6 months of age. An average Indian woman secretes about 750 ml of milk per day during the first 6 months and 600 ml/day subsequently upto one year. Many essential components are in concentrated amounts in colostrum as compared to mature milk, compensating for the low output during early lactation.

Breast-milk provides good quality proteins, fat, vitamins, calcium, iron and other minerals even beyond four months. In fact, its quality can be improved by supplementing the diet of the mother with nutrients. Growth of breast-fed infants is satisfactory upto 4-6 months of age.

When to start breast feeding and how long to continue ?

Mother-infant contact should be established as early as possible (immediately after birth) by permitting the infant to suck at the breast. Mothers can breast-feed from as early as 30 minutes after delivery. Colostrum should be made available to the infant immediately after birth. Feeding honey, glucose, water or dilute milk formula before lactation should be avoided and the infant should be allowed to suck, which helps in establishing lactation. Colostrum should not be discarded, as is sometimes practised.

The wrong way of feeding a baby.
Always feed in a sitting position.

Breast-feeding in India is common among the rural and urban poor, being less so among the urban middle and upper classes. The poorer groups continue breast-feeding for longer duration than the educated upper and middle income groups. The economically advantaged or the working mother, tends to discontinue breast-feeding early. A baby should be exclusively breast-fed only upto 4-6 months and supplementary foods should be introduced thereafter. Breast-feeding can be continued as long as possible, even upto 2 years. Demand feeding helps in maintaining lactation for a long time. If babies are quiet or sleep for 2 hours after a feed and show adequate weight gain, feeding may be assumed as adequate. Breast-fed infants do not need additional water. Feeding unsafe water increases the risk of diarrhoea and and should, therefore, be avoided.

What are the effects of maternal malnutrition on breast-milk ?

Composition of breast-milk depends to some extent on maternal nutrition. In general, even the undernourished mothers can successfully breast-feed. But in the case of severe malnutrition, both the quality and quantity of breast-milk may be affected. Protein content of breast-milk appears to be much less affected as compared to fat in malnutrition. Concentration of water-soluble vitamins, vitamin A (and beta-carotene) are influenced by the quality of the maternal diet. Administration of supplements of vitamins A and B-complex to lactating mothers increases the levels of these vitamins in breast-milk. Calcium and iron content can be increased in breast-milk by providing respective supplements to the mother. Also, iron from breast-milk is better absorbed. Trace element composition of breast-milk, however, is not affected by the mother's nutritional status.

How does breast-milk protect against infection ?

Diseases and death among breast-fed infants are much lower than those among formulated infants. Breast-feeding protects against diarrhoea and upper respiratory tract infections. The bifidus factor in breast-milk promotes the natural gut flora. The gut flora and the low pH of breast-milk inhibit the growth of pathogens. Breast-milk has immunoglobulins (IgA), lactoferrin, lactoperoxidase and complements which protect the infant from several infections. Antibodies to E-cofi and some viruses are found in breast milk, which protect the gut mucosa. Breast-feeding also protects infants from vulnerability to allergic reactions.

What ensures an adequate supply of breast-milk ?

It is necessary that the woman is emotionally prepared during pregnancy for breast-feeding and is encouraged to eat a well-balanced diet. Anxiety and emotional upset must be avoided and adequate rest should be ensured. It is necessary to prepare the breast, particularly the nipple, for breast-feeding. Mother should accept the baby for breast-feeding as early as possible after delivery and feed the child on demand.

Are drugs secreted in breast-milk ?

Since drugs (antibiotics, caffeine, hormones and alcohol) are secreted into the breastmilk and could prove harmful to the breast-fed infant, caution should be exercised by the lactating mother.

Breast feeding :

- ☞ Start breast-feeding within an hour after delivery and do not discard colostrum.
- ☞ Breast-feed exclusively for a minimum of four to six months.
- ☞ Continue breast-feeding even after introducing of supplements (weaning foods), upto 2 years.
- ☞ Breast-feed the infant frequently or on demand to establish and maintain good milk supply.
- ☞ Take a nutritionally adequate diet both during pregnancy and lactation.
- ☞ Avoid tobacco (smoking and chewing), alcohol and drugs during lactation.
- ☞ Ensure active family support for breast-feeding.

Food Supplement for Infants

What are supplements ?

Foods that are regularly fed to the infant, in addition to breast-milk, providing sufficient nutrients are known as supplementary or complementary foods. These could be liquids like milk or semi-solids like 'kheer'in the case of infants, or solid preparations like rice etc., in the case of children over the age of one year.

Why use supplements and when ?

At birth, mother's milk alone is adequate for the infant. Requirements of all the nutrients progressively increase with the infant's growth. Simultaneously, the breast-milk secretion in the mother comes down with time. Thus, infants are deprived of adequate nutrients due to the dual factors of increased nutrient requirements and decreased availability of breastmilk. Usually, these changes occur at about 4-6 months of age. Hence, promotion of optimal growth in infants, calls for introduction of adequate food supplements in addition to continued breast feeding, from the age of 4-6 months onwards.

Can home-made recipes be nutritious supplements.

Low cost food supplements can be prepared at home from commonly used ingredients such as cereals (wheat, rice, ragi, jowar, bajra, etc.); pulses (grams/dhals), nuts and oilseeds (groundnut, sesame, etc.), oils (groundnut oil, sesame oil etc.) and sugar and jaggery. Such supplements are easily digested by all infants, including those with severe malnutrition. The impression that only the commercially available supplementary foods are nutritious, is not correct. Some examples of low cost weaning foods are given on pages 27-28.

What are the principles in preparing weaning food supplements?

Weaning foods based on cereal-pulse-nut and sugar/jaggery combinations will provide good quality protein, adequate calories and other protective nutrients. Since infants cannot consume bulky weaning food, in sufficient quantities, energy-rich foods like fats and sugars should be included in such preparations. Infants can also be fed green leafy vegetables (GLV), which are rich, yet inexpensive, sources of vitamins and minerals. However, greens should be well cleaned before cooking lest the infants develop loose motions. Dietary fibre in green leafy vegetables can, by itself, promote the bowel movements leading to loose motions in infants. Since GLV are rich in dietary fibre, it is advisable to initially feed only the juice of the GLV after cooking them properly. Infants should be introduced to different vegetables and fruits gradually. It should, however, be remembered that these dietary articles should be thoroughly cooked and mashed before feeding. In families which can afford them, egg yolk and meat soup can be introduced. At about one year of age, the child should share the family diet.

How to Feed a Young Infant

Infants cannot eat large quantities of food in one sitting at a given time. So, they should be fed small quantities at frequent intervals (5-6 times a day). Also, the food should be of semi-solid consistency for easy swallowing. When such semi-solid foods are offered initially, the infant tends to spit it out, This should not be mistaken as dislike for that food. The fact is that the young infant cannot achieve full coordination needed for the act of swallowing, and, hence, brings out the food by movements of its tongue. Physiological maturity of swallowing the semi-solid food develops when the food is regularly given every day.

It is important to ensure that hygienic practices are scrupulously followed. All the dietary ingredients should be thoroughly cleaned. Vegetables should be washed well to remove contaminants/parasites/pesticides before cutting. Vegetables should preferably be steamcooked to reduce cooking losses. At the time of preparation and feeding of the recipes, mother should observe proper personal hygiene and the utensils used for cooking should be thoroughly washed or sterilized, wherever possible. A number of pre-cooked and ready to-eat foods can be prepared for use as weaning foods (vide pages 27-28). Such foods should be stored in clean bottles or tins. As feeding is likely to be time consuming, the cup or the plate from which the recipe is being fed to the infant should be kept covered to protect it from flies. Most often, diarrhoea is caused by unhygienic practices adopted by mothers. The weaning foods which are properly cleaned and well-cooked are safe even for young infants.

Infants

- Breast-milk alone is not enough for infants after 4-6 months of age.
- Feed supplements to the infants starting from 4-6 months of age, but continue breast-feeding.
- Do not delay supplementation.
- Feed low-cost home-made weaning foods.
- Feed supplements 5-6 times a day.
- Provide fruits and well cooked vegetables.
- Observe hygienic practices while preparing and feeding the supplement.

What should be done if breast-milk is not adequate ?

- If breast-feeding fails, the infant needs to be fed animal milk or commercial infant formula.
- Milk should be boiled before being to the boy.
- To start with, milk may be diluted with an equal volume of water.
- Full strength milk may be started from 4 weeks of age.
- Infants fed animal milk should receive supplements of iron and vitamin C.
- About 120-180 ml of milk should be fed with one teaspoon of sugar per feed, 6-8 times over the day.
- While reconstituting the infant formula, the instructions given on the label should be strictly followed.
- The feeds should be prepared and given using a sterile cup, spoon, bottles and nipples, taking utmost care.
- Overfeeding should be avoided in artificially-fed infants to prevent obesity.

☞ Low-cost home-made weaning foods are preferred. However, commercially available preparation may be used by those who can afford them.

Weaning Foods

Kichidi :

Rice	-	30 g
Green gram dal	-	15 g
Leafy vegetable	-	2 tbsp
Fat	-	2 tbsp
Cumin (jeera)		

Method: Clean rice and dhal and cook them in water with salt till the grains are soft and water is absorbed. Leafy vegetables can be added when the cereal/pulse is 3/4th done. Cumin is fried in fat and added towards the end.

Malted Ragi Porridge

Malted Ragi	-	30 g
Roasted Groundnut	-	15 g
Jaggery	-	20 g

Method: Malted ragi, roasted groundnuts; and jaggery are powdered. Sufficient water is added and cooked.

Wheat Payasam

Wheat	-	30 g
Roasted Bengal gram flour	-	15 g
Roasted & crushed Groundnut	-	5 g
Sugar	-	15 g

Method: Roast whole wheat and powder. Add roasted Bengal gram flour, groundnut and sugar. Cook with sufficient water.

Kheer

Vermicelli / Rice	-	30 g
Milk	-	100 ml.
Water	-	As required
Jaggery	-	20 g

Method: Boil rice/vermicelli in water till half done. Add milk and bring to boil. Add jaggery and cook well.

Note :

1. All these recipes provide approximately 250 Kcals. and 5 g proteins and amounts given are for 2 servings.
2. Recipes Nos.2 and 3 can be prepared and stored in airtight containers to be used whenever required.
3. Non-vegetarian foods such as soft boiled egg, minced meat may be introduced at the age of 6 months.

Feeding of Infants During Ailments

During periods of infection, children tend to eat less due to reduced appetite. Many children vomit frequently. Nutrients are also lost in urine and faeces. The unhealthy practice of restricting diet, including breast-feeding, by the mother during any sickness could further aggravate the problem. Hence, extra care is needed in feeding the child appropriately during and after illness to prevent subsequent nutritional deficiencies.

How should a child be fed during illness ?

Breast-feeds are often well accepted and tolerated even by sick children and should be continued except in severe gastroenteritis associated with shock. For older children, consuming an adult diet, soft cooked food may be offered at frequent intervals. The quantity of the feeds may be increased, after the illness has subsided, till the original weight is regained.

What should be done during diarrhoea

Diarrhoea is a common childhood disease which leads to dehydration and sometimes death. The child requires prompt correction of fluid and electrolyte loss using oral rehydration solution (ORS) along with early feeding. ORS can be prepared by adding a pinch of salt (between thumb and finger) and a teaspoon of sugar to a glass of potable water. Home-made fluids such as rice kanji or buttermilk with salt can also be used. During infections, children should frequently be given small quantities of fluids by mouth, including plain water.

During diarrhoea, feeding should be continued, though this goes against the popular practice. Breast-milk promotes sodium and water transport across the gut and, thus, prevents dehydration and weight loss, in addition to providing other nutrients.

The diet of 1-2 year old children with diarrhoea should provide energy of about 1000 Kcal/day. Calorie-rich, semi-solid, soft diets may be prepared from a variety of cereals and pulses. Sprouted grains are easily digestible and provide good nutrition (vide page 24). Fat and sugar help in reducing the bulk of the diets. Milk may be mixed with cereal diet to avoid lactose malabsorption. If milk is not tolerated, it may be replaced by an equal volume of curd/yogurt. Mashed vegetables may be incorporated in the diet. Feeding becomes easier after the infection subsides. About 6-8 feeds should be given during the day so that the extra food (120-140 Kcal/kg) may be consumed by the child without any difficulty.

How important is the problem of lactose intolerance 9

Deficiency of the enzyme lactose leads to lactose intolerance (vide page 55). During acute or chronic diarrhoea, lactose intolerance is a mild and transient problem. This problem can be overcome by reducing the quantity of milk taken at a time or taking milk along with a cereal-pulse meal. There is no need to stop milk in acute diarrhoea. In chronic diarrhoea, some children may develop lactose intolerance. In such children, milk may be stopped temporarily. A diet based on cereals and pulses or chicken and egg white allows the gut to recover and milk can then be slowly introduced. Adequate feeding during and after diarrhoea prevents malnutrition.

Infant

- Feed small quantities of soft cooked cereal-pulse based diets in addition to breast milk during infancy.
- Take extra care in feeding a young child and include soft cooked vegetables and seasonal fruits.
- Give plenty of milk and milk products to children and asdolescents.
- Discourage overeating as well as indiscriminate dieting.

During Illness :

- Never starve the child.
- Feed energy-rich cereal-pulse diets with milk and mashed vegetables.
- Feed small quantities at frequent intervals.
- Continue breast-feeding.
- Give plenty of fluids during illness.
- Use oral rehydration solution to prevent and correct dehydration, during diarrhoea episodes.

Essential Nutrients for All

All foods are rich in various nutrients, as no single item is an all contained item that can give essential nutrients to a person to meet his daily requirements thereof. In order to have balanced diet, certain vegetables, fruits, cereals, dairy products, fruits, cereals, poultry products are required to be blended or not taken in isolation except when a particular situation demands.

Following nutrients are said to be essential ingredients of a balanced diet.

1. Carbohydrates (sugar, wheat, grains, jaggery, etc.)
2. Proteins (fish, grains, soyabeans, cheese, etc.)
3. Fats (saturated and unsaturated fats like butter, vegetable oils, etc.)
4. Vitamins (A, B-Complex, C, D, E,K etc.)
5. Minerals (Iron, calcium, phosphorus, manganese, potassium etc.)
6. Dietary Fibre

CARBOHYDRATES

These are components of oxygen, hydrogen and carbon. They provide energy and heat to our body. Sugar and starch are well known sources of energy, and both of them are present in green plants. Lack of carbohydrates causes weakness, run down condition, restlessness in the body, whereas its excess causes fatness (obesity). Liver retains carbohydrates in the form of glycogen which is released by it, as soon as body requires it to sustain energy. Excessive release of glycogen into blood stream can cause rise in sugar levels of the blood and deficient supply can often result in low sugar percentage in the blood, both being forms of diabetes known as hyper and hypoglycaemia respectively. A routine need of a person is 160 to 240 gms. of carbohydrates which often is liable to vary depending on health state of a person.

PROTEINS

Proteins are required for proper development of our body and the word protein means, first in importance. They are conglomerates of phosphorous, sulphur, carbon, oxygen, nitrogen, etc. and deficient supply of proteins to the body will compel the body to eat its own muscles. Adequate supply of proteins is very important in our body so that all vital organs do continue to function in a normal way. Main function of proteins is to grow, repair and maintain organs and tissues of the body. In order to facilitate assimilation of proteins the body releases amino acids which are more then 70 in numbers. Enzymes break the proteins into amino acids, which in turn help protein to get absorbed into the blood stream. Out of 70 animo acids, 10 are considered to be most essential and such essential amino acids are known as high quality proteins Pulses augment short supply of protein, received from cereals. Hence to get an added advantage, cereals should always be taken with pulses. Our skin, muscles, hormones and enzymes are composed of amino acids and hence their requirement is of permanent nature. So is the need for constant supply of proteins. In the absence or short supply of proteins to the body, one is liable to feel tired and weak, whereas their excess supply will vitiate our blood, as also let them rot in our instestines.

Daily requirement of protein or a person should be one gm. per kg. of body weight, but it may be ensured that quality of protein is not inferior or substandard. For vegetarians, soyabeans are capable of giving almost double the amount of protein which equal amount of fish can give.

FATS

Fats discharge the function of lubricating the body, apart from being the concentrated source of energy, providing essential fatty acids for the aforesaid purpose. Our body's fat requirement is met from oils, pure fats. Apart from that some oil seeds, nuts, soyabeans also supply fats. Pulses and cereals have meager percentage of fats. It is a myth and a misplaced conception to totally eliminate oils from our diet. In fact, fats form an essential part our diet, as overuse is a dangerous and risky as total lack of use.

All oils and fatty acids have three types of fatty acids. Saturated, (which are causative of high risk or cholesterol in blood, if taken in excess,) fatty acids; polyunsaturated acids do not raise cholesterol levels whereas monounsatuarated acids lower the level of cholesterol. Hydrogenated vanaspati oils are rich in saturated fatty acids and it also matters as to how and in what way they have been processed. Following table will clearly indicate the concentration of approximated quantity (percentage) in each variety of oil derived from various derivatives.

For a normal adult, daily consumption of fat from 25-35 gms. seems to be correct. Persons doing hard work would require higher quantity of fats which should mainly be had from polyunsaturated fats, preferably vegetables. Heat generated by fats is almost double the amount of energy generated by carbohydrates, when process of oxidation takes place in the body This energy is converted into body heat and muscular work. Patients who suffer from heart aliments, arteriosclerosis, high blood pressure or any other like disorder should avoid saturated fats and substitute them with polyunsaturated fats. They should also avoid lard, palms oil, cream, butter and oil. Instead they should lay stress on the use of skimmed milk and its by products.

Contraception

Any intervention to prevent pregnancy. Contraception can be achieved in many ways and a listing of contraceptive principles and various preventive methods follows.

- revent sperm formation. There is no way to do this yet, though hormonal methods are being studied. Keep sperm out of the semen by VASECTOMY (cutting, tying or otherwisc blocking the spermatic ducts that lead from the testes to the penis).
- Keep semen out of the vagina by abstinence, COITUS INTERRUPTUS (ejaculation outside the vagina), or by catching the semen in a condom.
- Keep semen out of the vagina when fertilization could occur by predicting when ovulation will take place and abstain from coitus for 7 days before and 2 days after that event, or by abstained from the beginning of menstruating until after ovulation. This method is called PERIODIC ABSTINENCE. The various ways of predicting ovulation include the Billings and other mucus methods, the basal temperate method, and the symptomatically (symptom and temperature) method.
- Kill sperm in the vagina by using SPERMICIDES.
- Prevent sperm from passing through the cervical canal into the uterus by inserting a SERVILE BARRIER (such as a diaphragm) or by using hormones, the mint contraceptive pill, hormonal implants, to change the

servile mucus so that it become semipermeable to sperm.

- ☞ Prevent sperm from reaching the ovum (egg) by cutting, tying or otherwise blocking the fallopian tubes, as in female tube ligation (STERILISATION). The INTRAUTERINE DEVICE (IUD) is now believed to work mainly by interfering with the movement of sperm through the uterus to the tube.
- ☞ Prevent ovum development release by using hormonal contraception (the contraceptive pill, injection or implants). This occurs naturally during breast-feeding.
- ☞ Prevent implantation of a fertilized ovum by administration of hormones ('morning-after' pill). Contraception, Emerges Morning Pills

There are two ways to prevent pregnancy from an isolated act of unprotected sexual intercourse. 'MORNING-AFTER' PILL The 'morning-after' pill is a short course of hormones (usually estrogen plus progestrone) that will prevent pregnancy if it commences within 72 hours of unprotected intercourse. If it is started later or if the course is not completed, the treatment may not be successful.

Q-A ON CONTRACEPTION

In which condition should vasectomy not be encouraged ?

Vasectomy should be avoided in the following cases :

1. When a man is equating his masculinity with fathering of the child.
2. When there are unresolved doubts and conflicts about the procedure and its outcome.
3. Under abnormal local conditions where surgery becomes difficult (infection, varicocele, large hydrolcele, inguinal hernia, scar tissues from trauma, burns or surgery).

Are there any complications after vasectomy ?

Yes, occasionally. They may be surgical, immunological

or psychological. Surgical complications include bleeding (scrotal) or infection. These complications usually occur a week later.

Immunological complications are extremely rare and no cause-and-effect relationship is known.

Psychological complications are common and occur chiefly because of indicate counseling prior to the operation.

What precautions should one take after vasectomy to prevent surgical complications?

An athletic supporter or a tight fitting jockey type underwear should be worn for a week to help relieve the sweeping and to support the scrotum, thereby parts, removing the misconception that touching the private parts is taboo. This activity also draws early attention to any local pathology and prevents the development of any interrogations, skin infection.

A man should clean the penis daily, especially after retracting the foreskin upto the base of the glans penis. A woman must wash her vagina in a direction away from the vagina and not towards it, to prevent faecal contamination of the vagina and urethra.

Should a virgin use a tampon ?

The use of tampons in a young woman should be encouraged as it affords an opportunity for her to become acquainted with her own sexual anatomy and to overcome any doubts regarding handling her genitals. Moreover, the gradual minimal stressing of the humanely opening prepares her for later intercourse without difficulty. It would also give the young lady a healthier attitude towards her menstrual periods. However, one should know that the hymen may rupture while using tampons and may cause problems in those who harbour the misconception that a virgin must have an intact hymen !

Should a woman use vaginal douches or deodorants ?

No. This is not necessary. In fact these items may cause

irritating, inflammation and may increase the risk of infection by lettering the vaginal flora. Often, women use deodorants to mask offensive vaginal odorous (usually secondary to infection). The cause must be determined and treated accordingly.

Can one indulge in intercourse during menses ?

Certainly. Sex during menstruation is absolutely safe. If both partners desire, they can most certainly indulge. Menstrual material is sterile. Many couples find coitus more enjoyable at this time mainly because there is freedom from possible pregnancy and also because of the enhanced pleasure due to a most vagina.

Many women are under the impression that intercourse during menses may lead to increase in bleeding. Women do report heavier bleeding initially but the duration is often shortened considerably and the rhythmic contractions of the uterus during orgasm help in evacuation of the menstrual material more rapidly. In fact, a satisfying sexual intercourse during the menstrual period reduces cramps and alleviates the feeling of heavy discomfort resulting from pelvic congestion.

Note : Some doctors do advise the use of condoms, especially in case of those women who do not keep their perineum clean. Menstrual material may become a rich source of culture medium for the growth of bacteria owing to its close proximity to the anus, and may facilitate an inflammatory reaction in the man's urethra.

Does the use of lubricants hamper conception ?

Yes, the use of lubricants while indulging in sexual intercourse may immobilize sperms and hamper conception.

Smart Women are More Fertile

A woman's fertility is as plain as the nose on her face- or more particularly her cheekbones, chin and skin- but not if she is wearing make up, scientists said.

Researchers at the University of Saint Andrews in Scotland made the claim after asking volunteers to rate pictures of 59 young women aged 19 to 25 for attractiveness, health and femininity.

Comparing the results to an analysis of the photographed women's levels of oestrogen, they found that those with high counts of the sex hormone were judged to be prettier by both male and female participants.

As result, they were more likely to catch the attention of the oposite sex.

"Women are effectively advertising their general fertility with their faces," said Miriam law Smith, a psychologist who led the study. "Our findings could explain why men universally seem to prefer feminine women's faces."

"In evolutionary terms, it makes sense for men to favour feminine, fertile women," she added." Those that did would have had more babies." Oestrogen has an impact on a girl's appearance during puberty, particularly on bone growth and skin texture.

Attractive bone structure and smooth skin were found

to correspond to high levels of the hormone. But no relationship was found between perceived appearance and oestrogen in the study's responses to women wearing make-up, suggesting cosmetics could be hiding fertility cues, the researchers said.

IMMUNIZATION

Get your child immunized as per this schedule :

Age of the Child	Vaccine to be given to the child	Number of doses	Profects against
6 weeks	Oral Polio vaccine (OPV)	1	Polio
	DPT	1	Diptheria Pertusis Tetanus
	BCG	1	Tuberculosis
10 weeks	OPV	1	Polio
	DPT	1	Diptheria Pertusis Tetanus
14 weeks	OPV	1	-do-
	DPT	1	-do-

●●●

23. Life Begins at 40 125/-
24. Alternative Therapies 125/-
25. How to Overcome Stress 125/-
26. Yoga Therapy 225/-
27. Obesity 125/-
28. Self Motivation 125/-
29. Yoga for Health and Relaxation 110/-
30. Women Disorders and Pregnancy 110/-
31. A Guide to Body Pains 110/-
32. Sex Education 125/-
33. Common Diseases and Cure 125/-
34. Pranayama for Better Life 125/-
35. Herbal Home Remedies 125/-
36. A Guide to Beauty & Skin Care 110/-
37. A Guide to Heart Care 110/-
38. A Guide to High Blood Pressure 110/-
39. Cancer Causes and Prevention 125/-
40. Nature Cure for Common Diseases 125/-
41. Good Health Through Food and Regimen 110/-
42. A Guide to Allergies 125/-
43. A Guide to Aging 95/-
44. Ayurveda for Health & Beauty 125/-

Lotus PRESS

Unit No. 220, Second Floor, 4735/22,
Prakash Deep Building, Ansari Road, Darya Ganj,
New Delhi - 110002, Ph.: 32903912, 23280047, 09811594448
E-mail: lotus_press@sify.com, www.lotuspress.co.in